ISBN: 9781407651293

Published by:
HardPress Publishing
8345 NW 66TH ST #2561
MIAMI FL 33166-2626

Email: info@hardpress.net
Web: http://www.hardpress.net

The Imaginary Invalid

by

Moliere (Poquelin)

TABLE OF CONTENTS

WITH SHORT INTRODUCTIONS AND EXPLANATORY NOTES..................i

PERSONS REPRESENTED..iii

ACT I.. 1

SCENE I. ARGAN (SITTING AT A TABLE, ADDING UP HIS
APOTHECARY'S BILL WITH COUNTERS).. 2

SCENE II. ARGAN, TOINETTE... 4

SCENE III. ARGAN, ANGELIQUE, TOINETTE................................... 6

SCENE IV. ANGELIQUE, TOINETTE...7

SCENE V. ARGAN, ANGELIQUE, TOINETTE...................................10

SCENE VI. BELINE, ARGAN..18

SCENE VII. ARGAN, BELINE, TOINETTE....................................... 20

SCENE VIII. ARGAN, BELINE.. 22

SCENE IX. MR. DE BONNEFOI, BELINE, ARGAN.......................... 23

SCENE X. ANGELIQUE, TOINETTE... 26

SCENE XI. BELINE (IN THE HOUSE), ANGELIQUE, TOINETTE.............. 27

ACT II..28

SCENE I. CLEANTE, TOINETTE..29

SCENE II. ARGAN, TOINETTE.. 30

SCENE III: ARGAN, CLEANTE, TOINETTE.....................................31

SCENE IV. ARGAN, ANGELIQUE, CLEANTE.................................. 33

SCENE V. ARGAN, ANGELIQUE, CLEANTE, TOINETTE....................34

SCENE VI. MR. DIAFOIRUS, THOMAS DIAFOIRUS, ARGAN,
ANGELIQUE, CLEANTE, TOINETTE, SERVANTS.............................. 35

SCENE VII. BELINE, ARGAN, ANGELIQUE MR. DIAFOIRUS, T. DIAFOIRUS, TOINETTE..45

SCENE VIII. ARGAN, BELINE, MR. DIAFOIRUS, T. DIAFOIRUS, TOINETTE..49

SCENE IX. ARGAN, MR. DIAFOIRUS, T. DIAFOIRUS, TOINETTE.............50

SCENE X. BELINE, ARGAN...52

SCENE XI. ARGAN, LOUISON..53

SCENE XII. BERALDE, ARGAN...58

ACT III...62

SCENE I. BERALDE, ARGAN, TOINETTE......................................63

SCENE II. BERALDE, TOINETTE..64

SCENE III. ARGAN, BERALDE..65

SCENE IV MR. FLEURANT, ARGAN, BERALDE.................................72

SCENE V ARGAN, BERALDE...73

SCENE VI. MR. PURGON, ARGAN, BERALDE, TOINETTE.......................74

SCENE VII ARGAN, BERALDE..78

SCENE VIII. ARGAN, TOINETTE, BERALDE..................................79

SCENE IX. ARGAN, BERALDE..80

SCENE X. ARGAN, BERALDE, TOINETTE (DRESSED AS A DOCTOR)..............81

SCENE XI. ARGAN, BERALDE..82

SCENE XII. ARGAN, BERALDE, TOINETTE...................................83

SCENE XIII. ARGAN, BERALDE..84

SCENE XIV. ARGAN, BERALDE, TOINETTE (AS A DOCTOR)....................85

SCENE XV. ARGAN, BERALDE..90

SCENE XVI. ARGAN, BERALDE, TOINETTE..91

SCENE XVII. ARGAN, TOINETTE..93

SCENE XVIII. BELINE, ARGAN (STRETCHED OUT IN HIS CHAIR), TOINETTE..94

SCENE XIX. BERALDE (COMING OUT OF THE PLACE WHERE HE WAS HIDING), ARGAN, TOINETTE...96

SCENE XX. ARGAN, ANGELIQUE, TOINETTE..97

SCENE XXI. ARGAN, ANGELIQUE, CLEANTE, TOINETTE.........................98

SCENE XXII. ARGAN, BERALDE, ANGELIQUE, CLEANTE, TOINETTE..99

SCENE XXIII. BERALDE, ANGELIQUE, CLEANTE....................................101

WITH SHORT INTRODUCTIONS AND EXPLANATORY NOTES.

BY

CHARLES HERON WALL.

This is the last comedy written by Moliere. He was very ill, nearly dying, at the time he wrote it. It was first acted at the Palais Royal Theatre, on February 10, 1673.

Moliere acted the part of Argan.

PERSONS REPRESENTED.

ARGAN, *an imaginary invalid.*

BELINE, *second wife to* ARGAN.

ANGELIQUE, *daughter to* ARGAN, *in love with* CLEANTE.

LOUISON; ARGAN'S *young daughter, sister to* ANGELIQUE.

BERALDE, *brother to* ARGAN.

CLEANTE, *lover to* ANGELIQUE.

MR. DIAFOIRUS, *a physician.*

THOMAS DIAFOIRUS, *his son, in love with* ANGELIQUE.

MR. PURGON, *physician to* ARGAN.

MR. FLEURANT, *an apothecary.*

MR. DE BONNEFOI, *a notary.*

TOINETTE, *maid-servant to* ARGAN.

ACT I.

SCENE I. ARGAN (*sitting at a table, adding up his apothecary's bill with counters*).

ARG. Three and two make five, and five make ten, and ten make twenty. "Item, on the 24th, a small, insinuative clyster, preparative and gentle, to soften, moisten, and refresh the bowels of Mr. Argan." What I like about Mr. Fleurant, my apothecary, is that his bills are always civil. "The bowels of Mr. Argan." All the same, Mr. Fleurant, it is not enough to be civil, you must also be reasonable, and not plunder sick people. Thirty sous for a clyster! I have already told you, with all due respect to you, that elsewhere you have only charged me twenty sous; and twenty sous, in the language of apothecaries, means only ten sous. Here they are, these ten sous. "Item, on the said day, a good detergent clyster, compounded of double catholicon rhubarb, honey of roses, and other ingredients, according to the prescription, to scour, work, and clear out the bowels of Mr. Argan, thirty sons." With your leave, ten sous. "Item, on the said day, in the evening, a julep, hepatic, soporiferous, and somniferous, intended to promote the sleep of Mr. Argan, thirty-five sous." I do not complain of that, for it made me sleep very well. Ten, fifteen, sixteen, and seventeen sous six deniers. "Item, on the 25th, a good purgative and corroborative mixture, composed of fresh cassia with Levantine senna and other ingredients, according to the prescription of Mr. Purgon, to expel Mr. Argan's bile, four francs." You are joking, Mr. Fleurant; you must learn to be reasonable with patients; Mr. Purgon never ordered you to put four francs. Tut! put three francs, if you please. Twenty; thirty sous. [Footnote: As usual, Argan only counts half; even after he has reduced the charge.] "Item, on the said day, a dose, anodyne and astringent, to make Mr. Argan sleep, thirty sous." Ten sous, Mr. Fleurant. "Item, on the 26th, a carminative clyster to cure the flatulence of Mr. Argan, thirty sous." "Item, the clyster repeated in the evening, as above, thirty sous." Ten sous, Mr. Fleurant. "Item, on the 27th, a good mixture composed for the purpose of driving out the bad humours of Mr. Argan, three francs." Good; twenty and thirty sous; I am glad that you are reasonable. "Item, on the 28th, a dose of clarified and edulcorated whey, to soften, lenify, temper, and refresh the blood of Mr. Argan, twenty sous." Good; ten sous. "Item, a potion, cordial and preservative, composed of twelve grains of bezoar, syrup of citrons and pomegranates, and other ingredients, according to the prescription, five francs." Ah! Mr. Fleurant, gently, if you please; if you go on like that, no one will wish to be unwell. Be satisfied with four francs. Twenty, forty sous. Three and two are five, and five are ten, and ten are twenty. Sixty-three francs four sous six deniers. So that during this month I have taken one, two, three, four, five, six, seven, eight mixtures, and one, two, three, four, five, six, seven, eight, nine, ten, eleven, twelve clysters; and last month there were twelve mixtures and twenty clysters. I am not astonished, therefore, that I am not so well this month as last. I shall speak to Mr. Purgon about it, so that he may set the matter right. Come, let all this be taken away. (*He sees that no one comes, and that he is alone.*) Nobody. It's no use, I am always left alone; there's no way of keeping them here. (*He rings a hand-bell.*) They don't hear, and my bell doesn't make enough noise. (*He rings again.*) No one. (*He rings again.*) Toinette! (*He rings again.*) It's just as if I didn't ring at all. You hussy! you jade! (*He rings again.*) Confound it all! (*He rings and shouts.*) Deuce take you, you wretch!

SCENE II. ARGAN, TOINETTE.

TOI. Coming, coming.

ARG. Ah! you jade, you wretch!

TOI. (*pretending to have knocked her head*). Bother your
impatience! You hurry me so much that I have knocked my head against
the window-shutter.

ARG. (*angry*). You vixen!

TOI. (*interrupting* ARGAN). Oh!

ARG. There is....

TOI. Oh!

ARG. For the last hour I....

TOI. Oh!

ARG. You have left me....

TOI. Oh!

ARG. Be silent! you baggage, and let me scold you.

TOI. Well! that's too bad after what I have done to myself.

ARG. You make me bawl till my throat is sore, you jade!

TOI. And you, you made me break my head open; one is just as bad as
the other; so, with your leave, we are quits.

ARG. What! you hussy....

TOI. If you go on scolding me, I shall cry.

4

ARG. To leave me, you....

TOI. (*again interrupting* ARGAN.) Oh!

ARG. You would....

TOI. (*still interrupting him*). Oh!

ARG. What! shall I have also to give up the pleasure of scolding her?

TOI. Well, scold as much as you please; do as you like.

ARG. You prevent me, you hussy, by interrupting me every moment.

TOI. If you have the pleasure of scolding, I surely can have that of crying. Let every one have his fancy; 'tis but right. Oh! oh!

ARG. I must give it up, I suppose. Take this away, take this away, you jade. Be careful to have some broth ready, for the other that I am to take soon.

TOI. This Mr. Fleurant and Mr. Purgon amuse themselves finely with your body. They have a rare milch-cow in you, I must say; and I should like them to tell me what disease it is you have for them to physic you so.

ARG. Hold your tongue, simpleton; it is not for you to control the decrees of the faculty. Ask my daughter Angelique to come to me. I have something to tell her.

TOI. Here she is, coming of her own accord; she must have guessed your thoughts.

SCENE III. ARGAN, ANGELIQUE, TOINETTE.

ARG. You come just in time; I want to speak to you.

ANG. I am quite ready to hear you.

ARG. Wait a moment. (*To* TOINETTE) Give me my walking-stick; I'll come back directly.

TOI. Go, Sir, go quickly; Mr. Fleurant gives us plenty to do.

SCENE IV. ANGELIQUE, TOINETTE.

ANG. Toinette!

TOI. Well! what?

ANG. Look at me a little.

TOI. Well, I am looking at you.

ANG. Toinette!

TOI. Well! what, Toinette?

ANG. Don't you guess what I want to speak about?

TOI. Oh! yes, I have some slight idea that you want to speak of our
young lover, for it is of him we have been speaking for the last six
days, and you are not well unless you mention him at every turn.

ANG. Since you know what it is I want, why are you not the first to
speak to me of him? and why do you not spare me the trouble of being
the one to start the conversation?

TOI. You don't give me time, and you are so eager that it is difficult
to be beforehand with you on the subject.

ANG. I acknowledge that I am never weary of speaking of him, and that
my heart takes eager advantage of every moment I have to open my heart
to you. But tell me, Toinette, do you blame the feelings I have
towards him?

TOI. I am far from doing so.

ANG. Am I wrong in giving way to these sweet impressions?

TOI. I don't say that you are.

ANG. And would you have me insensible to the tender protestations of ardent love which he shows me?

TOI. Heaven forbid!

ANG. Tell me, do you not see, as I do, Something providential, some act of destiny in the unexpected adventure from which our acquaintance originated?

TOI. Yes.

ANG. That it is impossible to act more generously?

TOI. Agreed.

ANG. And that he did all this with the greatest possible grace?

TOI. Oh! yes.

ANG. Do you not think, Toinette, that he is very handsome?

TOI. Certainly.

ANG. That he has the best manners in the world?

TOI. No doubt about it.

ANG. That there is always something noble in what he says and what he does?

TOI. Most certainly.

ANG. That there never was anything more tender than all he says to me?

TOI. True.

ARG. And that there can be nothing more painful than the restraint under which I am kept? for it prevents all sweet intercourse, and puts an end to that mutual love with which Heaven has inspired us.

TOI. You are right.

ANG. But, dear Toinette, tell me, do you think that he loves me as much as he says he does?

TOI. Hum! That's a thing hardly to be trusted at any time. A show of love is sadly like the real thing, and I have met with very good actors in that line.

ANG. Ah! Toinette, what are you saying there? Alas! judging by the manner in which he speaks, is it possible that he is not telling the truth?

TOI. At any rate, you will soon be satisfied on this point, and the resolution which he says he has taken of asking you in marriage, is a sure and ready way of showing you if what he says is true or not. That is the all-sufficient proof.

ANG. Ah! Toinette, if he deceives me, I shall never in all my life believe in any man.

TOI. Here is your father coming back.

SCENE V. ARGAN, ANGELIQUE, TOINETTE.

ARG. I say, Angelique, I have a piece of news for yon which, perhaps, you did not expect. You have been asked of me in marriage. Halloa! how is that? You are smiling. It is pleasant, is it not, that word marriage? there is nothing so funny to young girls. Ah! nature! nature! So, from what I see, daughter, there is no need of my asking you if you are willing to marry.

ANG. I ought to obey you in everything, father.

ARG. I am very glad to possess such an obedient daughter; the thing is settled then, and I have promised you.

ANG. It is my duty, father, blindly to follow all you determine upon for me.

ARG. My wife, your mother-in-law, wanted me to make a nun of you and of your little sister Louison also. She has always been bent upon that.

TOI. (*aside*). The excellent creature has her reasons.

ARG. She would not consent to this marriage; but I carried the day, and my word is given.

TOI. (*to* ARGAN). Really, I am pleased with you for that, and it is the wisest thing you ever did in your life.

ARG. I have not seen the person in question; but I am told that I shall be satisfied with him, and that you too will be satisfied.

ANG. Most certainly, father.

ARG. How! have you seen him then?

ANG. Since your consent to our marriage authorises me to open my heart to you, I will not hide from you that chance made us acquainted six days ago, and that the request which has been made to you is the result of the sympathy we felt for one another at first sight.

ARG. They did not tell me that; but I am glad of it; it is much better that things should be so. They say that he is a tall, well-made young fellow.

ANG. Yes, father.

ARG. Of a fine build.

ANG. Yes, indeed.

ARG. Pleasant.

ANG. Certainly.

ARG. A good face.

ANG. Very good.

ARG. Steady and of good family.

ANG. Quite.

ARG. With very good manners.

ANG. The best possible.

ARG. And speaks both Latin and Greek.

ANG. Ah! that I don't know anything about.

ARG. And that he will in three days be made a doctor.

ANG. He, father?

ARG. Yes; did he not tell you?

ANG. No, indeed! who told you?

ARG. Mr. Purgon.

ANG. Does Mr. Purgon know him?

ARG. What a question! Of course he knows him, since he is his nephew.

ANG. Cleante is the nephew of Mr. Purgon?

ARG. What Cleante? We are speaking about him who has asked you in marriage.

ANG. Yes, of course.

ARG. Well, he is the nephew of Mr. Purgon, and the son of his brother-in-law, Mr. Diafoirus; and this son is called Thomas Diafoirus, and not Cleante. Mr. Fleurant and I decided upon this match this morning, and to-morrow this future son-in-law will be brought to me by his father ...What is the matter, you look all scared?

ANG. It is because, father, I see that you have been speaking of one person, and I of another.

TOI. What! Sir, you have formed such a queer project as that, and, with all the wealth you possess, you want to marry your daughter to a doctor?

ARG. What business is it of yours, you impudent jade?

TOI. Gently, gently. You always begin by abuse. Can we not reason together without getting into a rage? Come, let us speak quietly. What reason have you, if you please, for such a marriage?

ARG. My reason is, that seeing myself infirm and sick, I wish to have a son-in-law and relatives who are doctors, in order to secure their kind assistance in my illness, to have in my family the fountain-head of those remedies which are necessary to me, and to be within reach of consultations and prescriptions.

TOI. Very well; at least that is giving a reason, and there is a certain pleasure in answering one another calmly. But now, Sir, on your conscience, do you really and truly believe that you are ill?

ARG. Believe that I am ill, you jade? Believe that I am ill, you impudent hussy?

TOI. Very well, then, Sir, you are ill; don't let us quarrel about that. Yes, you are very ill, I agree with you upon that point, more ill even than you think. Now, is that settled? But your daughter is to marry a husband for herself, and as she is not ill, what is the use of giving her a doctor?

ARG. It is for my sake that I give her this doctor, and a good daughter ought to be delighted to marry for the sake of her father's health.

TOI. In good troth, Sir, shall I, as a friend, give you a piece of advice?

ARG. What is this advice?

TOI. Not to think of this match.

ARG. And your reason?

TOI. The reason is that your daughter will never consent to it.

ARG. My daughter will not consent to it?

TOI. No.

ARG. My daughter?

TOI. Your daughter. She will tell you that she has no need of Mr. Diafoirus, nor of his son, Mr. Thomas Diafoirus, nor all the Diafoiruses in the world.

ARG. But I have need of them. Besides, the match is more advantageous than you think. Mr. Diafoirus has only this son for his heir; and, moreover, Mr. Purgon, who has neither wife nor child, gives all he has in favour of this marriage; and Mr. Purgon is a man worth eight thousand francs a year.

TOI. What a lot of people he must have killed to have become so rich!

ARG. Eight thousand francs is something, without counting the property of the father.

TOI. That is very well, Sir, but, all the same, I advise you, between ourselves, to choose another husband for her; she is not of a make to become a Mrs. Diafoirus.

ARG. But I will have it so.

TOI. Fie! nonsense! Don't speak like that.

ARG. Don't speak like that? Why not?

TOI. Dear me, no, don't.

ARG. And why should I not speak like that?

TOI. People will say that you don't know what you are talking about.

ARG. People will say all they like, but I tell you that I will have her make my promise good.

TOI. I feel sure that she won't.

ARG. Then I will force her to do it.

TOI. She will not do it, I tell you.

ARG. She will, or I will shut her up in a convent

TOI. You?

ARG. I.

TOI. Good!

ARG. How good?

TOI. You will not shut her up in a convent.

ARG. I shall not shut her up in a convent?

TOI. No.

ARG. No?

TOI. No.

ARG. Well, this is cool! I shall not put my daughter in a convent if I like!

TOI. No, I tell you.

ARG. And who will hinder me?

TOI. You yourself.

ARG. Myself?

TOI. You will never have the heart to do it.

ARG. I shall.

TOI. You are joking.

ARG. I am not joking.

TOI. Fatherly love will hinder you.

ARG. It will not hinder me.

TOI. A little tear or two, her arms thrown round your neck, Or "My darling little papa." said very tenderly, will be enough to touch your heart.

ARG. All that will be useless.

TOI. Oh yes!

ARG. I tell you that nothing will move me.

TOI. Rubbish!

ARG. You have no business to say "Rubbish."

TOI. I know you well enough; you are naturally kind-hearted.

ARG. (*angrily*). I am not kind-hearted, and I am ill-natured
when I like.

TOI. Gently, Sir, you forget that you are ill.

ARG. I command her to prepare herself to take the husband I have fixed
upon.

TOI. And I decidedly forbid her to do anything of the kind.

ARG. What have we come to? And what boldness is this for a scrub of a
servant to speak in such a way before her master?

TOI. When a master does not consider what he is doing, a sensible
servant should set him right.

ARG. (*running after* TOINETTE). Ah, impudent girl, I will kill
you!

TOI. (*avoiding* ARGAN, *and putting the chair between her and
him*). It is my duty to oppose what would be a dishonour to you.

ARG. (*running after* TOINETTE *with his cane in his hand*).
Come here, come here, let me teach you how to speak.

TOI. (*running to the opposite side of the chair*). I interest
myself in your affairs as I ought to do, and I don't wish to see you
commit any folly.

ARG. (*as before*). Jade!

16

TOI. (*as before*). No, I will never consent to this marriage.

ARG. (*as before*). Worthless hussy!

TOI. (*as before*). I won't have her marry your Thomas Diafoirus.

ARG. (*as before*). Vixen!

TOI. (*as before*). She will obey me sooner than you.

ARG. (*stopping*). Angelique, won't you stop that jade for me?

ANG. Ah! father, don't make yourself ill.

ARG. (*to* ANGELIQUE). If you don't stop her, I will refuse you my blessing.

TOI. (*going away*). And I will disinherit her if she obeys you.

ARG. (*throwing himself into his chair*). Ah! I am done for. It is enough to kill me!

SCENE VI. BELINE, ARGAN.

ARG. Ah! come near, my wife.

BEL. What ails you, my poor, dear husband?

ARG. Come to my help.

BEL. What is the matter, my little darling child?

ARG. My love.

BEL. My love.

ARG. They have just put me in a rage.

BEL. Alas! my poor little husband! How was that, my own dear pet?

ARG. That jade of yours, Toinette, has grown more insolent than ever.

BEL. Don't excite yourself.

ARG. She has put me in a rage, my dove.

BEL. Gently, my child.

ARG. She has been thwarting me for the last hour about everything I want to do.

BEL. There, there; never mind.

ARG. And has had the impudence to say that I am not ill.

BEL. She is an impertinent hussy.

ARG. You know, my soul, what the truth is?

BEL. Yes, my darling, she is wrong.

18

ARG. My own dear, that jade will be the death of me.

BEL. Now, don't, don't.

ARG. She is the cause of all my bile.

BEL. Don't be so angry.

ARG. And I have asked you ever so many times to send her away.

BEL. Alas! my child, there is no servant without defects. We are obliged to put up at times with their bad qualities on account of their good ones. The girl is skilful, careful, diligent, and, above all, honest; and you know that in our days we must be very careful what people we take into our house. I say, Toinette.

SCENE VII. ARGAN, BELINE, TOINETTE.

TOI. Madam.

BEL. How is this? Why do you put my husband in a passion?

TOI. (*in a soft tone*). I, Madam? Alas! I don't know what you mean, and my only aim is to please master in everything.

ARG. Ah! the deceitful girl!

TOI. He said to us that he wished to marry his daughter to the son of Mr. Diafoirus. I told him that I thought the match very advantageous for her, but that I believed he would do better to put her in a convent.

BEL. There is not much harm in that, and I think that she is right.

ARG. Ah! deary, do you believe her? She is a vile girl, and has said a hundred insolent things to me.

BEL. Well, I believe you, my dear. Come, compose yourself; and you, Toinette, listen to me. If ever you make my husband angry again, I will send you away. Come, give me his fur cloak and some pillows, that I may make him comfortable in his arm-chair. You are all anyhow. Pull your night-cap right down over your ears; there is nothing that gives people such bad colds as letting in the air through the ears.

ARG. Ah, deary! how much obliged I am to you for all the care you take of me.

BEL. (*adjusting the pillows, which she puts round him*). Raise yourself a little for me to put this under you. Let us put this one for you to lean upon, and this one on the other side; this one behind your back, and this other to support your head.

TOI. (*clapping a pillow rudely on his head*). And this other to keep you from the evening damp.

ARG. (*rising angrily, and throwing the pillows after* TOINETTE, *who runs away*). Ah, wretch! you want to smother me.

SCENE VIII. ARGAN, BELINE.

BEL. Now, now; what is it again?

ARG. (*throwing himself in his chair*). Ah! I can hold out no
longer.

BEL. But why do you fly into such a passion? she thought she was doing
right.

ARG. You don't know, darling, the wickedness of that villainous
baggage. She has altogether upset me, and I shall want more than eight
different mixtures and twelve injections to remedy the evil.

BEL. Come, come, my dearie, compose yourself a little.

ARG. Lovey, you are my only consolation.

BEL. Poor little pet!

ARG. To repay you for all the love you have for me, my darling, I
will, as I told you, make my will.

BEL. Ah, my soul I do not let us speak of that, I beseech you. I
cannot bear to think of it, and the very word "will" makes me die of
grief.

ARG. I had asked you to speak to our notary about it.

BEL. There he is, close at hand; I have brought him with me.

ARG. Make him come in then, my life!

BEL. Alas! my darling, when a woman loves her husband so much, she
finds it almost impossible to think of these things.

SCENE IX. MR. DE BONNEFOI, BELINE, ARGAN.

ARG. Come here, Mr. de Bonnefoi, come here. Take a seat, if you please. My wife tells me, Sir, that you are a very honest man, and altogether one of her friends; I have therefore asked her to speak to you about a will which I wish to make.

BEL. Alas! I cannot speak of those things.

MR. DE BON. She has fully explained to me your intentions, Sir, and what you mean to do for her. But I have to tell you that you can give nothing to your wife by will.

ARG. But why so?

MR. DE BON. It is against custom. If you were in a district where statute law prevailed, the thing could he done; but in Paris, and in almost all places governed by custom, it cannot be done; and the will would be held void. The only settlement that man and wife can make on each other is by mutual donation while they are alive, and even then there must be no children from either that marriage or from any previous marriage at the decease of the first who dies.

ARG. It's a very impertinent custom that a husband can leave nothing to a wife whom he loves, by whom he is tenderly loved, and who takes so much care of him. I should like to consult my own advocate to see what I can do.

MR. DE BON. It is not to an advocate that you must apply; for they are very particular on this point and think it a great crime to bestow one's property contrary to the law. They are people to make difficulties, and are ignorant of the bylaws of conscience. There are others whom you may consult with advantage on that point, and who have expedients for gently overriding the law, and for rendering just that which is not allowed. These know how to smooth over the difficulties of an affair, and to find the means of eluding custom by some indirect advantage. Without that, what would become of us every day? We must make things easy; otherwise we should do nothing, and I wouldn't give a penny for our business.

ARG. My wife had rightly told me, Sir, that you were a very clever and honest man. What can I do, pray, to give her my fortune and deprive my children of it?

MR. DE BON. What you can do? You can discreetly choose a friend of your wife, to whom you will give all you own in due form by your will, and that friend will give it up to her afterwards; or else you can sign a great many safe bonds in favour of various creditors who will lend their names to your wife, and in whose hands they will leave a declaration that what was done was only to serve her. You can also in your lifetime put in her hands ready money and bills which you can make payable to bearer.

BEL. Alas! you must not trouble yourself about all that. If I lose you, my child, I will stay no longer in the world.

ARG. My darling!

BEL. Yes, my pet, if I were unfortunate enough to lose you....

ARG. My dear wifey!

BEL. Life would be nothing to me.

ARG. My love!

BEL. And I would follow you to the grave, to show you all the tenderness I feel for you.

ARG. You will break my heart, deary; comfort yourself, I beseech you.

MR. DE BON. (*to* BELINE). These tears are unseasonable; things have not come to that yet.

BEL. Ah, Sir! you don't know what it is to have a husband one loves tenderly.

ARG. All the regret I shall have, if I die, my darling, will be to have no child from you. Mr. Purgon told me he would make me have one.

MR. DE BON. That may come still.

ARG. I must make my will, deary, according to what this gentleman advises; but, out of precaution, I will give you the twenty thousand francs in gold which I have in the wainscoting of the recess of my room, and two bills payable to bearer which are due to me, one from Mr. Damon, the other from Mr. Geronte.

BEL. No, no! I will have nothing to do with all that. Ah! How much do you say there is in the recess?

ARG. Twenty thousand francs, darling.

BEL. Don't speak to me of your money, I beseech you. Ah! How much are the two bills for?

ARG. One, my love, is for four thousand francs, and the other for six thousand.

BEL. All the wealth in the world, my soul, is nothing to me compared to you.

MR. DE BON. (*to* ARGAN). Shall we draw up the will?

ARG. Yes, Sir. But we shall be more comfortable in my own little study. Help me, my love.

BEL. Come, my poor, dear child.

SCENE X. ANGELIQUE, TOINETTE.

TOI. They are shut up with the notary, and I heard something about a will; your mother-in-law doesn't go to sleep; it is, no doubt, some conspiracy of hers against your interests to which she is urging your father.

ANG. Let him dispose of his money as he likes, as long as be does not dispose of my heart in the same way. You see, Toinette, to what violence it is subjected. Do not forsake me, I beseech you, in this my extremity.

TOI. I forsake you! I had rather die. In vain does your stepmother try to take me into her confidence, and make me espouse her interests. I never could like her, and I have always been on your side. Trust me, I will do every thing to serve you. But, in order to serve you more effectually, I shall change my tactics, hide my wish to help you, and affect to enter into the feelings of your father and your stepmother.

ANG. Try, I beseech you, to let Cleante know about the marriage they have decided upon.

TOI. I have nobody to employ for that duty but the old usurer Punchinello, my lover; it will cost me a few honeyed words. which I am most willing to spend for you. To-day it is too late for that, but to-morrow morning early I will send for him, and he will be delighted to....

SCENE XI. BELINE (*in the house*), ANGELIQUE, TOINETTE.

BEL. Toinette.

TOI. (*to* ANGELIQUE). I am called away. Good night. Trust me.

FIRST INTERLUDE.

ACT II.

SCENE I. CLEANTE, TOINETTE.

TOI. (*not recognising* CLEANTE). What is it you want, Sir?

CLE. What do I want?

TOI. Ah! ah! is it you? What a surprise! What are you coming here for?

CLE. To learn my destiny, to speak to the lovely Angelique, to consult the feelings of her heart, and to ask her what she means to do about this fatal marriage of which I have been told.

TOI. Very well; but no one speaks so easily as all that to Angelique; you must take precautions, and you have been told how narrowly she is watched. She never goes out, nor does she see anybody. It was through the curiosity of an old aunt that we obtained leave to go to the play where your love began, and we have taken good care not to say anything about it.

CLE. Therefore am I not here as Cleante, nor as her lover, but as the friend of her music-master, from whom I have obtained leave to say that I have come in his stead.

TOI. Here is her father; withdraw a little, and let me tell him who you are.

SCENE II. ARGAN, TOINETTE.

ARG. (*thinking himself alone*). Mr. Purgon told me that I was to walk twelve times to and fro in my room every morning, but I forgot to ask him whether it should be lengthways or across.

TOI. Sir, here is a gentleman....

ARG. Speak in a lower tone, you jade; you split my head open; and you forget that we should never speak so loud to sick people.

TOI. I wanted to tell you, Sir....

ARG. Speak low, I tell you.

TOI. Sir...(*She moves her lips as if she were speaking.*)

ARG. What?

TOI. I tell you that...(*As before.*)

ARG. What is it you say?

TOI. (*aloud*). I say that there is a gentleman here who wants to speak to you.

ARG. Let him come in.

SCENE III: ARGAN, CLEANTE, TOINETTE.

CLE. Sir.

TOI. (*to* CLEANTE). Do not speak so loud, for fear of splitting open the head of Mr. Argan.

CLE. Sir, I am delighted to find you up, and to see you better.

TOI. (*affecting to be angry*). How! better? It is false; master is always ill.

CLE. I had heard that your master was better, and I think that he looks well in the face.

TOI. What do you mean by his looking well in the face? He looks very bad, and it is only impertinent folks who say that he is better; he never was so ill in his life.

ARG. She is right.

TOI. He walks, sleeps, eats, and drinks, like other folks, but that does not hinder him from being very ill.

ARG. Quite true.

CLE. I am heartily sorry for it, Sir. I am sent by your daughter's music-master; he was obliged to go into the country for a few days, and as I am his intimate friend, he has asked me to come here in his place, to go on with the lessons, for fear that, if they were discontinued, she should forget what she has already learnt.

ARG. Very well. (To TOINETTE) Call Angelique.

TOI. I think, Sir, It would be better to take the gentleman to her room.

ARG. No, make her come here.

TOI. He cannot give her a good lesson if they are not left alone.

ARG. Oh! yes, he can.

TOI. Sir, it will stun you; and you should have nothing to disturb you in the state of health you are in.

ARG. No, no; I like music, and I should be glad to...Ah! here she is. (*To* TOINETTE) Go and see if my wife is dressed.

SCENE IV. ARGAN, ANGELIQUE, CLEANTE.

ARG. Come, my daughter, your music-master is gone into the country, and here is a person whom he sends instead, to give you your lesson.

ANG. (*recognising* CLEANTE). O heavens!

ARG. What is the matter? Why this surprise?

ANG. It is....

ARG. What can disturb you in that manner?

ANG. It is such a strange coincidence.

ARG. How so?

ANG. I dreamt last night that I was in the greatest trouble imaginable, and that some one exactly like this gentleman came to me. I asked him to help me, and presently he saved me from the great trouble I was in. My surprise was very great to meet unexpectedly, on my coming here, him of whom I had been dreaming all night.

CLE. It is no small happiness to occupy your thoughts whether sleeping or waking, and my delight would be great indeed if you were in any trouble out of which you would think me worthy of delivering you. There is nothing that I would not do for....

SCENE V. ARGAN, ANGELIQUE, CLEANTE, TOINETTE.

TOI. (*to* ARGAN). Indeed, Sir, I am of your opinion now, and I unsay all that I said yesterday. Here are Mr. Diafoirus the father, and Mr. Diafoirus the son, who are coming to visit you. How well provided with a son-in-law you will be! You will see the best-made young fellow in the world, and the most intellectual. He said but two words to me, it is true, but I was struck with them, and your daughter will be delighted with him.

ARG. (*to* CLEANTE, *who moves as if to go*). Do not go, Sir. I am about, as you see, to marry my daughter, and they have just brought her future husband, whom she has not as yet seen.

CLE. You do me great honour, Sir, in wishing me to be witness of such a pleasant interview.

ARG. He is the son of a clever doctor, and the marriage will take place in four days.

CLE. Indeed!

ARG. Please inform her music-master of it, that he may be at the wedding.

CLE. I will not fail to do so.

ARG. And I invite you also.

CLE. You do me too much honour.

TOI. Come, make room; here they are.

SCENE VI. MR. DIAFOIRUS, THOMAS DIAFOIRUS, ARGAN, ANGELIQUE, CLEANTE, TOINETTE, SERVANTS.

ARG. (*putting up his hand to his night-cap without taking it off*). Mr. Purgon has forbidden me to uncover my head. You belong to the profession, and know what would be the consequence if I did so.

MR. DIA. We are bound in all our visits to bring relief to invalids, and not to injure them.

(MR. ARGAN *and* MR. DIAFOIRUS *speak at the same time.*)

ARG. I receive, Sir....

MR. DIA. We come here, Sir....

ARG. With great joy....

MR. DIA. My son Thomas and myself....

ARG. The honour you do me....

MR. DIA. To declare to you, Sir....

ARG. And I wish....

MR. DIA. The delight we are in....

ARG. I could have gone to your house....

MR. DIA. At the favour you do us....

ARG. To assure you of it....

MR. DIA. In so kindly admitting us....

ARG. But you know, Sir....

MR. DIA. To the honour, Sir....

ARG. What it is to be a poor invalid....

MR. DIA. Of your alliance....

ARG. Who can only....

MR. DIA. And assure you....

ARG. Tell you here....

MR. DIA. That in all that depends on our knowledge....

ARG. That he will seize every opportunity....

MR. DIA. As well as in any other way....

ARG. To show you, Sir....

MR. DIA: That we shall ever be ready, Sir....

ARG. That he is entirely at your service....

MR. DIA. To show you our zeal. (*To his son*) Now, Thomas, come forward, and pay your respects.

T. DIA. (*to* MR. DIAFOIRUS). Ought I not to begin with the father?

MR. DIA. Yes.

T. DIA. (*to* ARGAN). Sir, I come to salute, acknowledge, cherish, and revere in you a second father; but a second father to whom I owe more, I make bold to say, than to the first. The first gave me birth; but you have chosen me. He received me by necessity, but you have accepted me by choice. What I have from him is of the body, corporal; what I hold from you is of the will, voluntary; and in so much the more as the mental faculties are above the corporal, in so much the more do I hold precious this future affiliation, for which I come beforehand to-day to render you my most humble and most respectful homage.

TOI. Long life to the colleges which send such clever people into the world!

T. DIA. (*to* MR. DIAFOIRUS). Has this been said to your satisfaction, father?

MR. DIA. *Optime.*

ARG. (*to* ANGELIQUE). Come, bow to this gentleman.

T DIA. (*to* MR. DIAFOIRUS). Shall I kiss?

MR. DIA. Yes, yes.

T. DIA. (*to* ANGELIQUE). Madam, it is with justice that heaven has given you the name of stepmother, since we see in you steps towards the perfect beauty which....[Footnote: Thomas Diafoirus is evidently going to base some compliment on the *belle-mere*. The only way out of the difficulty in English seems to be to complete the sentence somewhat.]

ARG. (*to* THOMAS DIAFOIRUS). It is not to my wife, but to my daughter, that you are speaking.

T. DIA. Where is she?

ARG. She will soon come.

T. DIA. Shall I wait, father, till she comes?

MR. DIA. No; go through your compliments to the young lady in the meantime.

T. DIA. Madam, as the statue of Memnon gave forth a harmonious sound when it was struck by the first rays of the sun, in like manner do I experience a sweet rapture at the apparition of this sun of your beauty. As the naturalists remark that the flower styled heliotrope always turns towards the star of day, so will my heart for ever turn towards the resplendent stars of your adorable eyes as to its only pole. Suffer me, then, Madam, to make to-day on the altar of your charms the offering of a heart which longs for and is ambitious of no greater glory than to be till death, Madam, your most humble, most obedient, most faithful servant and husband.

TOI. Ah! See what it is to study, and how one learns to say fine things!

ARG. (*to* CLEANTE). Well! what do you say to that?

CLE. The gentleman does wonders, and if he is as good a doctor as he is an orator, it will be most pleasant to be one of his patients.

TOI. Certainly, it will be something admirable if his cures are as wonderful as his speeches.

ARG. Now, quick, my chair; and seats for everybody. (*Servants bring chairs.*) Sit down here, my daughter. (*To* MR. DIAFOIRUS) You see, Sir, that everybody admires your son; and I think you very fortunate in being the father of such a fine young man.

MR. DIA. Sir, it is not because I am his father, but I can boast that I have reason to be satisfied with him, and that all those who see him speak of him as of a youth without guile. He has not a very lively imagination, nor that sparkling wit which is found in some others; but it is this which has always made me augur well of his judgment, a quality required for the exercise of our art. As a child he never was what is called sharp or lively. He was always gentle, peaceful, taciturn, never saying a word, and never playing at any of those little pastimes that we call children's games. It was found most difficult to teach him to read, and he was nine years old before he knew his letters. A good omen, I used to say to myself; trees slow of growth bear the best fruit. We engrave on marble with much more difficulty than on sand, but the result is more lasting; and that dulness of apprehension, that heaviness of imagination, is a mark of a sound judgment in the future. When I sent him to college, he found it hard work, but he stuck to his duty, and bore up with obstinacy against all difficulties. His tutors always praised him for his assiduity and the trouble he took. In short, by dint of continual hammering, he at last succeeded gloriously in obtaining his degree; and I can say, without vanity, that from that time till now there has been no candidate who has made more noise than he in all the disputations of our school. There he has rendered himself formidable, and no debate passes but be goes and argues loudly and to the last extreme on the opposite side. He is firm in dispute, strong as a Turk in his principles, never changes his opinion, and pursues an argument to the last recesses of logic. But, above all things, what pleases me in him, and what I am glad to see him follow my example in, is that he is blindly attached to the opinions of the ancients, and that he would never understand nor listen to the reasons and the experiences of the pretended discoveries of our century concerning the circulation of the blood and other opinions of the same stamp. [Footnote: Harvey's treatise on the circulation of the blood was published in 1628. His discovery was violently opposed for a long time afterwards.]

T. DIA. (*pulling out of his pocket a long paper rolled up, and presenting it to* ANGELIQUE). I have upheld against these circulators a thesis which, with the permission (*bowing to* ARGAN) of this gentleman, I venture to present to the young lady as the first-fruits of my genius.

ANG. Sir, it is a useless piece of furniture to me; I do not understand these things.

TOI. (*taking the paper*). Never mind; give it all the same; the picture will be of use, and we will adorn our attic with it.

T. DIA. (*again bowing to* ANGELIQUE). With the permission of this gentleman, I invite you to come one of these days to amuse yourself by assisting at the dissection of a woman upon whose body I am to give lectures.

TOI. The treat will be most welcome. There are some who give the pleasure of seeing a play to their lady-love; but a dissection is much more gallant.

MR. DIA. Moreover, in respect to the qualities required for marriage, I assure you that he is all you could wish, and that his children will be strong and healthy.

ARG. Do you not intend, Sir, to push his way at court, and obtain for him the post of physician there?

MR. DIA. To tell you the truth, I have never had any predilection to practice with the great; it never seemed pleasant to me, and I have found that it is better for us to confine ourselves to the ordinary public. Ordinary people are more convenient; you are accountable to nobody for your actions, and as long as you follow the common rules laid down by the faculty, there is no necessity to trouble yourself about the result. What is vexatious among people of rank is that, when they are ill, they positively expect their doctor to cure them.

TOI. How very absurd! How impertinent of them to ask of you doctors to cure them! You are not placed near them for that, but only to receive your fees and to prescribe remedies. It is their own look-out to get well if they can.

MR. DIA. Quite so. We are only bound to treat people according to form.

ARG. (*to* CLEANTE). Sir, please make my daughter sing before the company.

CLE. I was waiting for your commands, Sir; and I propose, in order to amuse the company, to sing with the young lady an operetta which has lately come out. (*To* ANGELIQUE, *giving her a paper*) There is your part.

ANG. Mine?

CLE. (*aside to* ANGELIQUE). Don't refuse, pray; but let me explain to you what is the scene we must sing. (*Aloud*) I have no voice; but in this case it is sufficient if I make myself understood; and you must have the goodness to excuse me, because I am under the necessity of making the young lady sing.

ARG. Are the verses pretty?

CLE. It is really nothing but a small extempore opera, and what you will hear is only rhythmical prose or a kind of irregular verse, such as passion and necessity make two people utter.

ARG. Very well; let us hear.

CLE. The subject of the scene is as follows. A shepherd was paying every attention to the beauties of a play, when he was disturbed by a noise close to him, and on turning round he saw a scoundrel who, with insolent language, was annoying a young shepherdess. He immediately espoused the cause of a sex to which all men owe homage; and after having chastised the brute for his insolence, he came near the shepherdess to comfort her. He sees a young girl with the most beautiful eyes he has ever beheld, who is shedding tears which he thinks the most precious in the world. Alas! says he to himself, can any one be capable of insulting such charms? Where is the unfeeling wretch, the barbarous man to be found who will not feel touched by such tears? He endeavours to stop those beautiful tears, and the lovely shepherdess takes the opportunity of thanking him for the slight service he has rendered her. But she does it in a manner so touching, so tender, and so passionate that the shepherd cannot resist it, and each word, each look is a burning shaft which penetrates his heart. Is there anything in the world worthy of such thanks? and what will not one do, what service and what danger will not one be delighted to run to attract upon oneself even for a moment the touching sweetness of so grateful a heart? The whole play was acted without his paying any more attention to it; yet he complains that it was too short, since the end separates him from his lovely shepherdess. From that moment, from that first sight, he carries away with him a love which has the strength of a passion of many years. He now feels all the pangs of absence, and is tormented in no longer seeing what he beheld for so short a time. He tries every means to meet again with a sight so dear to him, and the remembrance of which pursues him day and night. But the great watch which is kept over his shepherdess deprives him of all the power of doing so. The violence of his passion urges him to ask in marriage the adorable beauty without whom he can no longer live, and he obtains from her the permission of doing so, by means of a note that he has succeeded in sending to her. But he is told in the meantime that the father of her whom he loves has decided upon marrying her to another, and that everything is being got ready to celebrate the wedding. Judge what a cruel wound for the heart of that poor shepherd! Behold him suffering from this mortal blow; he cannot bear the dreadful idea of seeing her he loves in the arms of another; and in his despair he finds the means of introducing himself into the house of his shepherdess, in order to learn her feelings and to hear from her the fate he must expect. There he sees everything ready for what he fears; he sees the unworthy rival whom the caprice of a father opposes to the tenderness of his love; he sees that ridiculous rival triumphant near the lovely shepherdess, as if already assured of his conquest. Such a sight fills him with a wrath he can hardly master. He looks despairingly at her whom he adores, but the respect he has for her and the presence of her father prevent him from speaking except with his eyes. At last he breaks through all restraint, and the greatness of his love forces him to speak as follows.

(*He sings.*)

Phyllis, too sharp a pain you bid me bear;
Break this stern silence, tell me what to fear;
Disclose your thoughts, and bid them open lie
To tell me if I live or die.

ANG.
The marriage preparations sadden me.
O'erwhelmed with sorrow,
My eyes I lift to heaven; I strive to pray,
Then gaze on you and sigh. No more I say.

CLE.
Tircis, who fain would woo,

42

Tell him, Phyllis, is it true,
Is he so blest by your sweet grace
As in your heart to find a place?

ANG.
I may not hide it, in this dire extreme,
Tircis, I own for you my love....

CLE.
O blessed words! am I indeed so blest?
Repeat them, Phyllis; set my doubts at rest.

ANG.
I love you, Tircis!

CLE.
Ah! Phyllis, once again.

ANG.
I love you, Tircis!

CLE.
Alas! I fain
A hundred times would hearken to that strain.

ANG.
I love you! I love you!
Tircis, I love you!

CLE.
Ye kings and gods who, from your eternal seat,
Behold the world of men beneath your feet,
Can you possess a happiness more sweet?
My Phyllis! one dark haunting fear
Our peaceful joy disturbs unsought;
A rival may my homage share.

ANG.
Ah! worse than death is such a thought!

Its presence equal torment is
To both, and mars my bliss.

CLE. Your father to his vow would subject you.

ANG. Ah! welcome death before I prove untrue.

ARG. And what does the father say to all that?

CLE. Nothing.

ARG. Then that father is a fool to put up with those silly things,
without saying a word!

CLE. (*trying to go on singing*).
Ah! my love....

ARG. No; no; that will do. An opera like that is in very bad taste.
The shepherd Tircis is an impertinent fellow, and the shepherdess
Phyllis an impudent girl to speak in that way in the presence of her
father. (*To* ANGELIQUE) Show me that paper. Ah! ah! and where
are the words that you have just sung? This is only the music.

CLE. Are you not aware, Sir, that the way of writing the words with
the notes themselves has been lately discovered?

ARG. Has it? Good-bye for the present. We could have done very well
without your impertinent opera.

CLE. I thought I should amuse you.

ARG. Foolish things do not amuse, Sir. Ah! here is my wife.

SCENE VII. BELINE, ARGAN, ANGELIQUE MR. DIAFOIRUS, T. DIAFOIRUS, TOINETTE.

ARG. My love, here is the son of Mr. Diafoirus.

T. DIA. Madam, it is with justice that heaven has given you the title of stepmother, since we see in you steps....

BEL. Sir, I am delighted to have come here just in time to see you.

T. DIA. Since we see in you...since we see in you ...Madam, you have interrupted me in the middle of my period, and have troubled my memory.

MR. DIA. Keep it for another time.

ARG. I wish, my dear, that you had been here just now.

TOI. Ah! Madam, how much you have lost by not being at the second father, the statue of Memnon, and the flower styled heliotrope.

ARG. Come, my daughter, shake hands with this gentleman, and pledge him your troth.

ANG. Father!

ARG. Well? What do you mean by "Father"?

ANG. I beseech you not to be in such a hurry; give us time to become acquainted with each other, and to see grow in us that sympathy so necessary to a perfect union.

T. DIA. As far as I am concerned, Madam, it is already full-grown within me, and there is no occasion for me to wait.

ANG. I am not so quick as you are, Sir, and I must confess that your

45

merit has not yet made enough impression on my heart.

ARG. Oh! nonsense! There will be time enough for the impression to be made after you are married.

ANG. Ah! my father, give me time, I beseech you! Marriage is a chain which should never be imposed by force. And if this gentleman is a man of honour, he ought not to accept a person who would be his only by force.

T. DIA. *Nego consequentiam.* I can be a man of honour, Madam, and at the same time accept you from the hands of your father.

ANG. To do violence to any one is a strange way of setting about inspiring love.

T. DIA. We read in the ancients, Madam, that it was their custom to carry off by main force from their father's house the maiden they wished to marry, so that the latter might not seem to fly of her own accord into the arms of a man.

ANG. The ancients, Sir, are the ancients; but we are the moderns. Pretences are not necessary in our age; and when a marriage pleases us, we know very well how to go to it without being dragged by force. Have a little patience; if you love me, Sir, you ought to do what I wish.

T. DIA. Certainly, Madam, but without prejudice to the interest of my love.

ANG. But the greatest mark of love is to submit to the will of her who is loved.

T. DIA. *Distinguo*, Madam. In what does not regard the possession of her, *concedo*; but in what regards it, *nego*.

TOI. (to ANGELIQUE). It is in vain for you to argue. This gentleman is bran new from college, and will be more than a match for you. Why resist, and refuse the glory of belonging to the faculty?

BEL. She may have some other inclination in her head.

ANG. If I had, Madam, it would be such as reason and honour allow.

ARG. Heyday! I am acting a pleasant part here!

BEL. If I were you, my child, I would not force her to marry; I know very well what I should do.

ANG. I know what you mean, Madam, and how kind you are to me; but it may be hoped that your advice may not be fortunate enough to be followed.

BEL. That is because well-brought-up and good children, like you, scorn to be obedient to the will of their fathers. Obedience was all very well in former times.

ANG. The duty of a daughter has its limits, Madam, and neither reason nor law extend it to all things.

BEL. Which means that your thoughts are all in favour of marriage, but that you will choose a husband for yourself.

ANG. If my father will not give me a husband I like, at least I beseech him not to force me to marry one I can never love.

ARG. Gentlemen, I beg your pardon for all this.

ANG. We all have our own end in marrying. For my part, as I only want a husband that I can love sincerely, and as I intend to consecrate my whole life to him, I feel bound, I confess, to be cautious. There are some who marry simply to free themselves from the yoke of their parents, and to be at liberty to do all they like. There are others, Madam, who see in marriage only a matter of mere interest; who marry only to get a settlement, and to enrich themselves by the death of those they marry. They pass without scruple from husband to husband, with an eye to their possessions. These, no doubt, Madam, are not so difficult to satisfy, and care little what the husband is like.

BEL. You are very full of reasoning to-day. I wonder what you mean by this.

ANG. I, Madam? What can I mean but what I say?

BEL. You are such a simpleton, my dear, that one can hardly bear with you.

ANG. You would like to extract from me some rude answer; but I warn you that you will not have the pleasure of doing so.

BEL. Nothing can equal your impertinence.

ANG. It is of no use, Madam; you will not.

BEL. And you have a ridiculous pride, an impertinent presumption, which makes you the scorn of everybody.

ANG. All this will be useless, Madam. I shall be quiet in spite of you; and to take away from you all hope of succeeding in what you wish, I will withdraw from your presence.

SCENE VIII. ARGAN, BELINE, MR. DIAFOIRUS, T. DIAFOIRUS, TOINETTE.

ARG. (*to* ANGELIQUE, *as she goes away*). Listen to me! Of two things, one. Either you will marry this gentleman or you will go into a convent. I give you four days to consider. (*To* BELINE) Don't be anxious; I will bring her to reason.

BEL. I am sorry to leave you, my child; but I have some important business which calls me to town. I shall soon be back.

ARG. Go, my darling; call upon the notary, and tell him to be quick about you know what.

BEL. Good-bye, my child.

ARG. Good-bye, deary.

SCENE IX. ARGAN, MR. DIAFOIRUS, T. DIAFOIRUS, TOINETTE.

ARG. How much this woman loves me; it is perfectly incredible.

MR. DIA. We shall now take our leave of you, Sir.

ARG. I beg of you, Sir, to tell me how I am.

MR. DIA. (*feeling* ARGAN'S *pulse*). Now, Thomas, take the other arm of the gentleman, so that I may see whether you can form a right judgment on his pulse. *Quid dicis?*

T. DIA. *Dico* that the pulse of this gentleman is the pulse of a man who is not well.

MR. DIA. Good.

T. DIA. That it is *duriusculus*, not to say *durus*.

MR. DIA. Very well.

T. DIA. Irregular.

MR. DIA. *Bene*.

T. DIA. And even a little caprizant.

MR. DIA. *Optime*.

T. DIA. Which speaks of an intemperance in the splenetic *parenchyma*; that is to say, the spleen.

MR. DIA. Quite right.

ARG. It cannot be, for Mr. Purgon says that it is my liver which is out of order.

MR. DIA. Certainly; he who says *parenchyma* says both one and the other, because of the great sympathy which exists between them through the means of the *vas breve*, of the *pylorus*, and often of the *meatus choledici*. He no doubt orders you to eat plenty of roast-meat.

ARG. No; nothing but boiled meat.

MR. DIA. Yes, yes; roast or boiled, it is all the same; he orders very wisely, and you could not have fallen into better hands.

ARG. Sir, tell me how many grains of salt I ought to put to an egg?

MR. DIA. Six, eight, ten, by even numbers; just as in medicines by odd numbers.

ARG. Good-bye, Sir; I hope soon to have the pleasure of seeing you again.

SCENE X. BELINE, ARGAN.

BEL. Before I go out, I must inform you of one thing you must be careful about. While passing before Angelique's door, I saw with her a young man, who ran away as soon as he noticed me.

ARG. A young man with my daughter!

BEL. Yes; your little girl Louison, who was with them, will tell you all about it.

ARG. Send her here, my love, send her here at once. Ah! the brazen-faced girl! (*Alone.*) I no longer wonder at the resistance she showed.

SCENE XI. ARGAN, LOUISON.

LOU. What do you want, papa? My step-mamma told me to come to you.

ARG. Yes; come here. Come nearer. Turn round, and hold up your head. Look straight at me. Well?

LOU. What, papa?

ARG. So?

LOU. What?

ARG. Have you nothing to say to me?

LOU. Yes. I will, to amuse you, tell you, if you like, the story of the Ass's Skin or the fable of the Fox and the Crow, which I have learnt lately.

ARG. That is not what I want of you.

LOU. What is it then?

ARG. Ah! cunning little girl, you know very well what I mean.

LOU. No indeed, papa.

ARG. Is that the way you obey me?

LOU. What, papa?

ARG. Have I not asked you to tell me at once all you see?

LOU. Yes, papa.

ARG. Have you done so?

LOU. Yes, papa. I always come and tell you all I see.

ARG. And have you seen nothing to-day?

LOU. No, papa.

ARG. No?

LOU. No, papa.

ARG. Quite sure?

LOU. Quite sure.

ARG. Ah! indeed! I will make you see something soon.

LOU. (*seeing* ARGAN *take a rod*). Ah! papa!

ARG. Ah! ah! false little girl; you do not tell me that you saw a man in your sister's room!

LOU. (*crying*). Papa!

ARG. (*taking* LOUISON *by the arm*). This will teach you to tell falsehoods.

LOU. (*throwing herself on her knees*). Ah! my dear papa! pray forgive me. My sister had asked me not to say anything to you, but I will tell you everything.

ARG. First you must have a flogging for having told an untruth. then we will see to the rest.

LOU. Forgive me, papa, forgive me!

ARG. No, no!

LOU. My dear papa, don't whip me.

ARG. Yes, you shall be whipped.

LOU. For pity's sake! don't whip me, papa.

ARG. (*going to whip her*). Come, come.

LOU. Ah! papa, you have hurt me; I am dead! (*She feigns to be dead.*)

ARG. How, now! What does this mean? Louison! Louison! Ah! heaven! Louison! My child! Ah! wretched father! My poor child is dead! What have I done? Ah! villainous rod! A curse on the rod! Ah! my poor child! My dear little Louison!

LOU. Come, come, dear papa; don't weep so. I am not quite dead yet.

ARG. Just see the cunning little wench. Well! I forgive you this once, but you must tell me everything.

LOU. Oh yes, dear papa.

ARG. Be sure you take great care, for here is my little finger that knows everything, and it will tell me if you don't speak the truth.

LOU. But, papa, you won't tell sister that I told you.

ARG. No, no.

LOU. (*after having listened to see if any one can hear*). Papa, a young man came into sister's room while I was there.

ARG. Well?

LOU. I asked him what he wanted; he said that he was her music-master.

ARG. (*aside*). Hm! hm! I see. (*To* LOUISON) Well?

LOU. Then sister came.

ARG. Well?

LOU. She said to him, "Go away, go away, go. Good heavens! you will drive me to despair."

ARG. Well?

LOU. But he would not go away.

ARG. What did he say to her?

LOU. Oh! ever so many things.

ARG. But what?

LOU. He told her this, and that, and the other; that he loved her dearly; that she was the most beautiful person in the world.

ARG. And then, after?

LOU. Then he knelt down before her.

ARG. And then?

LOU. Then he kept on kissing her hands.

ARG. And then?

LOU. Then my mamma came to the door, and, he escaped.

ARG. Nothing else?

LOU. No, dear papa.

ARG. Here is my little finger, which says something though. (*Putting his finger up to his ear.*) Wait. Stay, eh? ah! ah! Yes? oh! oh! here is my little finger, which says that there is something you saw, and which you do not tell me.

LOU. Ah! papa, your little finger is a story-teller.

ARG. Take care.

LOU. No, don't believe him; he tells a story, I assure you.

ARG. Oh! Well, well; we will see to that. Go away now, and pay great attention to what you see. (*Alone*.) Ah! children are no longer children nowadays! What trouble! I have not even enough leisure to attend to my illness. I am quite done up. (*He falls down into his chair.*)

SCENE XII. BERALDE, ARGAN.

BER. Well, brother! What is the matter? How are you?

ARG. Ah! very bad, brother; very bad.

BER. How is that?

ARG. No one would believe how very feeble I am.

BER. That's a sad thing, indeed.

ARG. I have hardly enough strength to speak.

BER. I came here, brother, to propose a match for my niece, Angelique.

ARG. (*in a rage, speaking with great fury, and starting up from his chair*). Brother, don't speak to me of that wicked, good-for-nothing, insolent, brazen-faced girl. I will put her in a convent before two days are over.

BER. Ah! all right! I am glad to see that you have a little strength still left, and that my visit does you good. Well, well, we will talk of business by-and-by. I have brought you an entertainment, which will dissipate your melancholy, and will dispose you better for what we have to talk about. They are gipsies dressed in Moorish clothes. They perform some dances mixed with songs, which, I am sure, you will like, and which will be as good as a prescription from Mr. Purgon. Come along.

SECOND INTERLUDE.

MEN *and* WOMEN (*dressed as Moors*).

FIRST MOORISH WOMAN.
When blooms the spring of life,
The golden harvest reap.
Waste not your years in bootless strife,

Till age upon your bodies creep.
But now, when shines the kindly light,
Give up your soul to love's delight.

No touch of sweetest joy
This longing heart can know,
No bliss without alloy
When love does silent show.

Then up, ye lads and lasses gay!
The spring of life is fair;
Cloud not these hours with care,
For love must win the day.

Beauty fades,
Years roll by,
Lowering shades
Obscure the sky.
And joys so sweet of yore
Shall charm us then no more.

Then up, ye lads and lasses gay!
The spring of life is fair;
Cloud not these hours with care,
For love must win the day.

First Entry of the BALLET.

2ND MOORISH WOMAN.
They bid us love, they bid us woo,
Why seek delay?
To tender sighs and kisses too
In youth's fair day,
Our hearts are but too true.

The sweetest charms has Cupid's spell.
No sooner felt, the ready heart
His conquered self would yield him well

Ere yet the god had winged his dart.
But yet the tale we often hear
Of tears and sorrows keen,
To share in them, I ween,
Though sweet, would make us fear!

3RD MOORISH WOMAN.
To love a lover true,
In youth's kind day, I trow,
Is pleasant task enow;
But think how we must rue
If he inconstant show!

4TH MOORISH WOMAN.
The loss of lover false to me
But trifling grief would be,
Yet this is far the keenest smart
That he had stol'n away our heart.

2ND MOORISH WOMAN.
What then shall we do
Whose hearts are so young?

4TH MOORISH WOMAN.
Though cruel his laws,
Attended by woes,
Away with your arms,
Submit to his charms!

TOGETHER.
His whims ye must follow,
His transports though fleet,
His pinings too sweet
Though often comes sorrow,
The thousand delights
The wounds of his darts
Still charm all the hearts.

* * * * *

ACT III.

SCENE I. BERALDE, ARGAN, TOINETTE.

BER. Well, brother, what do you say to that? Isn't it as good as a dose of cassia?

TOI. Oh! good cassia is a very good thing, Sir.

BER. Now, shall we have a little chat together.

ARG. Wait a moment, brother, I'll be back directly.

TOI. Here, Sir; you forget that you cannot get about without a stick.

ARG. Ay, to be sure.

SCENE II. BERALDE, TOINETTE.

TOI. Pray, do not give up the interest of your niece.

BER. No, I shall do all in my power to forward her wishes.

TOI. We must prevent this foolish marriage which he has got into his head, from taking place. And I thought to myself that it would be a good thing to introduce a doctor here, having a full understanding of our wishes, to disgust him with his Mr. Purgon, and abuse his mode of treating him. But as we have nobody to act that part for us, I have decided upon playing him a trick of my own.

BER. In what way?

TOI. It is rather an absurd idea, and it may be more fortunate than good. But act your own part. Here is our man.

SCENE III. ARGAN, BERALDE.

BER. Let me ask you, brother, above all things not to excite yourself during our conversation.

ARG. I agree.

BER. To answer without anger to anything I may mention.

ARG. Very well.

BER. And to reason together upon the business I want to discuss with you without any irritation.

ARG. Dear me! Yes. What a preamble!

BER. How is it, brother, that, with all the wealth you possess, and with only one daughter--for I do not count the little one--you speak of sending her to a convent?

ARG. How is it, brother, that I am master of my family, and that I can do all I think fit?

BER. Your wife doesn't fail to advise you to get rid, in that way, of your two daughters; and I have no doubt that, through a spirit of charity, she would be charmed to see them both good nuns.

ARG. Oh, I see! My poor wife again! It is she who does all the harm, and everybody is against her.

BER. No, brother; let us leave that alone. She is a woman with the best intentions in the world for the good of your family, and is free from all interested motives. She expresses for you the most extraordinary tenderness, and shows towards your children an inconceivable goodness. No, don't let us speak of her, but only of your daughter. What can be your reason for wishing to give her in marriage to the sort of a doctor?

ARG. My reason is that I wish to have a son-in-law who will suit my wants.

BER. But it is not what your daughter requires, and we have a more suitable match for her.

ARG. Yes; but this one is more suitable for me.

BER. But does she marry a husband for herself or for you, brother?

ARG. He must do both for her and for me, brother; and I wish to take into my family people of whom I have need.

BER. So that, if your little girl were old enough, you would give her to an apothecary?

ARG. Why not?

BER. Is it possible that you should always be so infatuated with your apothecaries and doctors, and be so determined to be ill, in spite of men and nature?

ARG. What do you mean by that, brother?

BER. I mean, brother, that I know of no man less sick than you, and that I should be quite satisfied with a constitution no worse than yours. One great proof that you are well, and that you have a body perfectly well made, is that with all the pains you have taken, you have failed as yet in injuring the soundness of your constitution, and that you have not died of all the medicine they have made you swallow.

ARG. But are you aware, brother, that it is these medicines which keep me in good health? Mr. Purgon says that I should go off if he were but three days without taking care of me.

BER. If you are not careful, he will take such care of you that he will soon send you into the next world.

ARG. But let us reason together, brother; don't you believe at all in medicine?

BER. No, brother; and I do not see that it is necessary for our salvation to believe in it.

ARG. What! Do you not hold true a thing acknowledged by everybody, and revered throughout all ages?

BER. Between ourselves, far from thinking it true, I look upon it as one of the greatest follies which exist among men; and to consider things from a philosophical point of view, I don't know of a more absurd piece of mummery, of anything more ridiculous, than a man who takes upon himself to cure another man.

ARG. Why will you not believe that a man can cure another?

BER. For the simple reason, brother, that the springs of our machines are mysteries about which men are as yet completely in the dark, and nature has put too thick a veil before our eyes for us to know anything about it.

ARG. Then, according to you, the doctors know nothing at all.

BER. Oh yes, brother. Most of them have some knowledge of the best classics, can talk fine Latin, can give a Greek name to every disease, can define and distinguish them; but as to curing these diseases, that's out of the question.

ARG. Still, you must agree to this, that doctors know more than others.

BER. They know, brother, what I have told you; and that does not effect many cures. All the excellency of their art consists in pompous gibberish, in a specious babbling, which gives you words instead of reasons, and promises instead Of results.

ARG. Still, brother, there exist men as wise and clever as you, and we see that in cases of illness every one has recourse to the doctor.

BER. It is a proof of human weakness, and not of the truth of their art.

ARG. Still, doctors must believe in their art, since they make use of it for themselves.

BER. It is because some of them share the popular error by which they themselves profit, while others profit by it without sharing it. Your Mr. Purgon has no wish to deceive; he is a thorough doctor from head to foot, a man who believes in his rules more than in all the demonstrations of mathematics, and who would think it a crime to question them. He sees nothing obscure in physic, nothing doubtful, nothing difficult, and through an impetuous prepossession, an obstinate confidence, a coarse common sense and reason, orders right and left purgatives and bleedings, and hesitates at nothing. We must bear him no ill-will for the harm he does us; it is with the best intentions in the world that he will send you into the next world, and in killing you he will do no more than he has done to his wife and children, and than he would do to himself, if need be. [Footnote: Moliere seems to refer to Dr. Guenaut, who was said to have killed with antimony (his favourite remedy) his wife, his daughter, his nephew, and two of his sons-in-law.--AIME MARTIN.]

ARG. It is because you have a spite against him. But let us come to the point. What is to be done when one is ill?

BER. Nothing, brother.

ARG. Nothing?

BER. Nothing. Only rest. Nature, when we leave her free, will herself gently recover from the disorder into which she has fallen. It is our anxiety, our impatience, which does the mischief, and most men die of their remedies, and not of their diseases.

ARG. Still you must acknowledge, brother, that we can in certain things help nature.

BER. Alas! brother; these are pure fancies, with which we deceive ourselves. At all times, there have crept among men brilliant fancies in which we believe, because they flatter us, and because it would be well if they were true. When a doctor speaks to us of assisting, succouring nature, of removing what is injurious to it, of giving it what it is defective in, of restoring it, and giving back to it the full exercise of its functions, when he speaks of purifying the blood, of refreshing the bowels and the brain, of correcting the spleen, of rebuilding the lungs, of renovating the liver, of fortifying the heart, of re-establishing and keeping up the natural heat, and of possessing secrets wherewith to lengthen life of many years--he repeats to you the romance of physic. But when you test the truth of what he has promised to you, you find that it all ends in nothing; it is like those beautiful dreams which only leave you in the morning the regret of having believed in them.

ARG. Which means that all the knowledge of the world is contained in your brain, and that you think you know more than all the great doctors of our age put together.

BER. When you weigh words and actions, your great doctors are two different kinds of people. Listen to their talk, they are the cleverest people in the world; see them at work, and they are the most ignorant.

ARG. Heyday! You are a great doctor, I see, and I wish that some one of those gentlemen were here to take up your arguments and to check your babble.

BER. I do not take upon myself, brother, to fight against physic; and every one at their own risk and peril may believe what he likes. What I say is only between ourselves; and I should have liked, in order to deliver you from the error into which you have fallen, and in order to amuse you, to take you to see some of Moliere's comedies on this subject.

ARG. Your Moliere is a fine impertinent fellow with his comedies! I think it mightily pleasant of him to go and take off honest people like the doctors.

BER. It is not the doctors themselves that he takes off, but the absurdity of medicine.

ARG. It becomes him well, truly, to control the faculty! He's a nice simpleton, and a nice impertinent fellow to laugh at consultations and prescriptions, to attack the body of physicians, and to bring on his stage such venerable people as those gentlemen.

BER. What would you have him bring there but the different professions of men? Princes and kings are brought there every day, and they are of as good a stock as your physicians.

ARG. No, by all the devils! if I were a physician, I would be revenged of his impertinence, and when he falls ill, I would let him die without relief. In vain would he beg and pray. I would not prescribe for him the least little bleeding, the least little injection, and I would tell him, "Die, die, like a dog; it will teach you to laugh at us doctors."

BER. You are terribly angry with him.

ARG. Yes, he is an ill-advised fellow, and if the doctors are wise, they will do what I say.

BER. He will be wiser than the doctors, for he will not go and ask their help.

ARG. So much the worse for him, if he has not recourse to their remedies.

BER. He has his reasons for not wishing to have anything to do with them; he is certain that only strong and robust constitutions can bear their remedies in addition to the illness, and he has only just enough strength for his sickness.

ARG. What absurd reasons. Here, brother, don't speak to me anymore about that man; for it makes me savage, and you will give me his complaint.

BAR. I will willingly cease, brother; and, to change the subject, allow me to tell you that, because your daughter shows a slight repugnance to the match you propose, it is no reason why you should shut her up in a convent. In your choice of a son-in-law you should not blindly follow the anger which masters you. We should in such a matter yield a little to the inclinations of a daughter, since it is for all her life, and the whole happiness of her married life depends on it.

SCENE IV MR. FLEURANT, ARGAN, BERALDE.

ARG. Ah! brother, with your leave.

BER. Eh? What are you going to do?

ARG. To take this little clyster; it will soon be done.

BER. Are you joking? Can you not spend one moment without clysters or physic? Put it off to another time, and be quiet.

ARG. Mr. Fleurant, let it be for to-night or to-morrow morning.

MR. FLEU. (to BERALDE). What right have you to interfere? How dare you oppose yourself to the prescription of the doctors, and prevent the gentleman from taking my clyster? You are a nice fellow to show such boldness.

BER. Go, Sir, go; it is easy to see that you are not accustomed to speak face to face with men.

MR. FLEU. You ought not thus to sneer at physic, and make me lose my precious time. I came here for a good prescription, and I will go and tell Mr. Purgon that I have been prevented from executing his orders, and that I have been stopped in the performance of my duty. You'll see, you'll see....

SCENE V-ARGAN, BERALDE.

ARG. Brother, you'll be the cause that some misfortune will happen here.

BER. What a misfortune not to take a clyster prescribed by Mr. Purgon! Once more, brother, is it possible that you can't be cured of this doctor disease, and that you will thus bring yourself under their remedies?

ARG. Ah! brother. You speak like a man who is quite well, but if you were in my place, you would soon change your way of speaking. It is easy to speak against medicine when one is in perfect health.

BER. But what disease do you suffer from?

ARG. You will drive me to desperation. I should like you to have my disease, and then we should see if you would prate as you do. Ah! here is Mr. Purgon.

SCENE VI. MR. PURGON, ARGAN, BERALDE, TOINETTE.

MR. PUR. I have just heard nice news downstairs! You laugh at my prescriptions, and refuse to take the remedy which I ordered.

ARG. Sir, it is not....

MR. PUR. What daring boldness, what a strange revolt of a patient against his doctor!

TOI. It is frightful.

MR. PUR. A clyster which I have had the pleasure of composing myself.

ARG. It was not I....

MR. PUR. Invented and made up according to all the rules of art.

TOI. He was wrong.

MR. PUR. And which was to work a marvellous effect on the intestines.

ARG. My brother....

MR. PUR. To send it back with contempt!

ARG. (*showing* BERALDE). It was he....

MR. PUR. Such conduct is monstrous.

TOI. So it is.

MR. PUR. It is a fearful outrage against medicine.

ARG. (*showing* BERALDE). He is the cause....

MR. PUR. A crime of high-treason against the faculty, and one which cannot be too severely punished.

TOI. You are quite right.

MR. PUR. I declare to you that I break off all intercourse with you.

ARG. It is my brother....

MR. PUR. That I will have no more connection with you.

TOI. You will do quite right.

MR. PUR. And to end all association with you, here is the deed of gift which I made to my nephew in favour of the marriage. (*He tears the document, and throws the pieces about furiously.*)

ARG. It is my brother who has done all the mischief.

MR. PUR. To despise my clyster!

ARG. Let it be brought, I will take it directly.

MR. PUR. I would have cured you in a very short time.

TOI. He doesn't deserve it.

MR. PUR. I was about to cleanse your body, and to clear it of its bad humours.

ARG. Ah! my brother

MR. PUR. And it wanted only a dozen purgatives to cleanse it entirely.

TOI. He is unworthy of your care.

MR. PUR. But since you would not be cured by me....

ARG. It was not my fault.

MR. PUR. Since you have forsaken the obedience you owe to your doctor....

TOI. It cries for vengeance.

MR. PUR. Since you have declared yourself a rebel against the remedies I had prescribed for you....

ARG. No, no, certainly not.

MR. PUR. I must now tell you that I give you up to your bad constitution, to the imtemperament of your intestines, to the corruption of your blood, to the acrimony of your bile, and to the feculence of your humours.

TOI. It serves you right.

ARG. Alas!

MR. PUR. And I will have you before four days in an incurable state.

ARG. Ah! mercy on me!

MR. PUR. You shall fall into bradypepsia.

ARG. Mr. Purgon!

MR. PUR. From bradypepsia into dyspepsia.

ARG. Mr. Purgon!

MR: PUR. From dyspepsia into apepsy.

ARG. Mr. Purgon!

MR. PUR. From apepsy into lientery.

ARG. Mr. Purgon!

MR. PUR. From lientery into dysentery.

ARG. Mr. Purgon!

MR. PUR. From dysentery into dropsy.

ARG. Mr. Purgon!

MR. PUR. And from dropsy to the deprivation of life into which your folly will bring you.

SCENE VII ARGAN, BERALDE.

ARG. Ah heaven! I am dead. Brother, you have undone me.

BER. Why? What is the matter?

ARG. I am undone. I feel already that the faculty is avenging itself.

BER. Really, brother, you are crazy, and I would not for a great deal that you should be seen acting as you are doing. Shake yourself a little, I beg, recover yourself, and do not give way so much to your imagination.

ARG. You hear, brother, with what strange diseases he has threatened me.

BER. What a foolish fellow you are!

ARG. He says that I shall become incurable within four days.

BER. And what does it signify what he says? Is it an oracle that has spoken? To hear you, anyone would think that Mr. Purgon holds in his hands the thread of your life, and that he has supreme authority to prolong it or to cut it short at his will. Remember that the springs of your life are in yourself, and that all the wrath of Mr. Purgon can do as little towards making you die, as his remedies can do to make you live. This is an opportunity, if you like to take it, of getting rid of your doctors; and if you are so constituted that you cannot do without them, it is easy for you, brother, to have another with whom you run less risk.

ARG. Ah, brother! he knows all about my constitution, and the way to treat me.

BER. I must acknowledge that you are greatly infatuated, and that you look at things with strange eyes.

SCENE VIII. ARGAN, TOINETTE, BERALDE.

TOI. (*to* ARGAN). There is a doctor, here, Sir, who desires to see you.

ARG. What doctor?

TOI. A doctor of medicine.

ARG. I ask you who he is?

TOI. I don't know who he is, but he is as much like me as two peas, and if I was not sure that my mother was an honest woman, I should say that this is a little brother she has given me since my father's death.

SCENE IX. ARGAN, BERALDE.

BER. You are served according to your wish. One doctor leaves you, another comes to replace him.

ARG. I greatly fear that you will cause some misfortune.

BER. Oh! You are harping upon that string again?

ARG. Ah! I have on my mind all those diseases that I don't understand, those....

SCENE X. ARGAN, BERALDE, TOINETTE (*dressed as a doctor*).

TOI. Allow me, Sir, to come and pay my respects to you, and to offer you my small services for all the bleedings and purging you may require.

ARG. I am much obliged to you, Sir. (*To* BERALDE) Toinette herself, I declare!

TOI. I beg you will excuse me one moment, Sir. I forgot to give a small order to my servant.

SCENE XI. ARGAN, BERALDE.

ARG. Would you not say that this is really Toinette?

BER. It is true that the resemblance is very striking. But it is not the first time that we have seen this kind of thing, and history is full of those freaks of nature.

ARG. For my part, I am astonished, and....

SCENE XII. ARGAN, BERALDE, TOINETTE.

TOI. What do you want, Sir?

ARG. What?

TOI. Did you not call me?

ARG. I? No.

TOI. My ears must have tingled then.

ARG. Just stop here one moment and see how much that doctor is like you.

TOI. Ah! yes, indeed, I have plenty of time to waste! Besides, I have seen enough of him already.

SCENE XIII. ARGAN, BERALDE.

ARG. Had I not seen them both together, I should have believed it was one and the same person.

BER. I have read wonderful stories about such resemblances; and we have seen some in our day that have taken in everybody.

ARG. For my part, I should have been deceived this time, and sworn that the two were but one.

SCENE XIV. ARGAN, BERALDE, TOINETTE (*as a doctor*).

TOI. Sir, I beg your pardon with all my heart.

ARG. (*to* BERALDE). It is wonderful.

TOI. You will not take amiss, I hope, the curiosity I feel to see such an illustrious patient; and your reputation, which reaches the farthest ends of the world, must be my excuse for the liberty I am taking.

ARG. Sir, I am your servant.

TOI. I see, Sir, that you are looking earnestly at me. What age do you think I am?

ARG. I should think twenty-six or twenty-seven at the utmost.

TOI. Ah! ah! ah! ah! ah! I am ninety years old.

ARG. Ninety years old!

TOI. Yes; this is what the secrets of my art have done for me to preserve me fresh and vigorous as you see.

ARG. Upon my word, a fine youthful old fellow of ninety!

TOI. I am an itinerant doctor, and go from town to town, from province to province, from kingdom to kingdom, to seek out illustrious material for my abilities; to find patients worthy of my attention, capable of exercising the great and noble secrets which I have discovered in medicine. I disdain to amuse myself with the small rubbish of common diseases, with the trifles of rheumatism, coughs, fevers, vapours, and headaches. I require diseases of importance, such as good non-intermittent fevers with delirium, good scarlet-fevers, good plagues, good confirmed dropsies, good pleurisies with inflammations of the lungs. These are what I like, what I triumph in, and I wish, Sir, that you had all those diseases combined, that you had been given up, despaired of by all the doctors, and at the point of death, so that I might have the pleasure of showing you the excellency of my remedies, and the desire I have of doing you service!

ARG. I am greatly obliged to you, Sir, for the kind intentions you have towards me.

TOI. Let me feel your pulse. Come, come, beat properly, please. Ah! I will soon make you beat as you should. This pulse is trifling with me; I see that it does not know me yet. Who is your doctor?

ARG. Mr. Purgon.

TOI. That man is not noted in my books among the great doctors. What does he say you are ill of?

ARG. He says it is the liver, and others say it is the spleen.

TOI. They are a pack of ignorant blockheads; you are suffering from the lungs.

ARG. The lungs?

TOI. Yes; what do you feel?

ARG. From time to time great pains in my head.

TOI. Just so; the lungs.

ARG. At times it seems as if I had a mist before my eyes.

TOI. The lungs.

ARG: I feel sick now and then.

TOI. The lungs.

ARG. And I feel sometimes a weariness in all my limbs.

TOI. The lungs.

ARG. And sometimes I have sharp pains in the stomach, as if I had the colic.

TOI. The lungs. Do you eat your food with appetite?

ARG. Yes, Sir.

TOI. The lungs. Do you like to drink a little wine?

ARG. Yes, Sir.

TOI. The lungs. You feel sleepy after your meals, and willingly enjoy a nap?

ARG. Yes, Sir.

TOI. The lungs, the lungs, I tell you. What does your doctor order you for food?

ARG. He orders me soup.

TOI. Ignoramus!

ARG. Fowl.

TOI. Ignoramus!

ARG. Veal.

TOI. Ignoramus!

ARG. Broth.

TOI. Ignoramus!

ARG. New-laid eggs.

TOI. Ignoramus!

ARG. And at night a few prunes to relax the bowels.

TOI. Ignoramus!

ARG. And, above all, to drink my wine well diluted with water.

TOI. *Ignorantus, ignoranta, ignorantum.* You must drink your
wine pure; and to thicken your blood, which is too thin, you must eat
good fat beef, good fat pork, good Dutch cheese, some gruel, rice
puddings, chestnuts, and thin cakes [Footnote: *Oublies*; now called
plaisirs. "Wafers" would perhaps have been the right rendering
in Moliere's time], to make all adhere and conglutinate. Your doctor
is an ass. I will send you one of my own school, and will come and
examine you from time to time during my stay in this town.

ARG. You will oblige me greatly.

TOI. What the deuce do you want with this arm?

ARG. What?

TOI. If I were you, I should have it cut off on the spot.

ARG. Why?

TOI. Don't you see that it attracts all the nourishment to itself, and
hinders this side from growing?

ARG. May be; but I have need of my arm.

TOI. You have also a right eye that I would have plucked out if I were
in your place.

ARG. My right eye plucked out?

TOI. Don't you see that it interferes with the other, and robs it of
its nourishment? Believe me; have it plucked out as soon as possible;
you will see all the clearer with the left eye.

ARG. There is no need to hurry.

TOI. Good-bye. I am sorry to leave you so soon, but I must assist at a grand consultation which is to take place about a man who died yesterday.

ARG. About a man who died yesterday?

TOI. Yes, that we may consider and see what ought to have been done to cure him. Good-bye.

ARG. You know that patients do not use ceremony.

SCENE XV. ARGAN, BERALDE.

BER. Upon my word, this doctor seems to be a very clever man.

ARG. Yes, but he goes a little too fast.

BER. All great doctors do so.

ARG. Cut off my arm and pluck out my eye, so that the other may be better. I had rather that it were not better. A nice operation indeed, to make me at once one-eyed and one-armed.

SCENE XVI. ARGAN, BERALDE, TOINETTE.

TOI. (*pretending to speak to somebody*). Come, come, I am your servant; I'm in no joking humour.

ARG. What is the matter?

TOI. Your doctor, forsooth, who wanted to feel my pulse!

ARG. Just imagine; and that, too, at fourscore and ten years of age.

BER. Now, I say, brother, since you have quarrelled with Mr. Purgon, won't you give me leave to speak of the match which is proposed for my niece?

ARG. No, brother; I will put her in a convent, since she has rebelled against me. I see plainly that there is some love business at the bottom of it all, and I have discovered a certain secret interview which they don't suspect me to know anything about.

BER. Well, brother, and suppose there were some little inclination, where could the harm be? Would it be so criminal when it all tends to what is honourable--marriage?

ARG. Be that as it may, she will be a nun. I have made up my mind.

BER. You intend to please somebody by so doing.

ARG. I understand what you mean. You always come back to that, and my wife is very much in your way.

BER. Well, yes, brother; since I must speak out, it is your wife I mean; for I can no more bear with your infatuation about doctors than with your infatuation about your wife, and see you run headlong into every snare she lays for you.

TOI. Ah! Sir, don't talk so of mistress. She is a person against whom there is nothing to be said; a woman without deceit, and who loves master--ah! who loves him...I can't express how much.

ARG. (*to* BERALDE). Just ask her all the caresses she lavishes for me.

TOI. Yes, indeed!

ARG. And all the uneasiness my sickness causes her.

TOI. Certainly.

ARG. And the care and trouble she takes about me.

TOI. Quite right. (*To* BERALDE) Will you let me convince you; and to show you at once how my mistress loves my master. (*To ARGAN*) Sir, allow me to undeceive him, and to show him his mistake.

ARG. How?

TOI. My mistress will soon come back. Stretch yourself full-length in this arm-chair, and pretend to be dead. You will see what grief she will be in when I tell her the news.

ARG. Very well, I consent.

TOI. Yes; but don't leave her too long in despair, for she might die of it.

ARG. Trust me for that.

TOI. (*to* BERALDE). Hide yourself in that corner.

SCENE XVII. ARGAN, TOINETTE.

ARG. Is there no danger in counterfeiting death?

TOI. No, no. What danger can there be? Only stretch yourself there. It will be so pleasant to put your brother to confusion. Here is my mistress. Mind you keep still.

SCENE XVIII. BELINE, ARGAN (*stretched out in his chair*), TOINETTE.

TOI. (*pretending not to see* BELINE). Ah heavens! Ah! what a misfortune! What a strange accident!

BEL. What is the matter, Toinette?

TOI. Ah! Madam!

BEL. What ails you?

TOI. Your husband is dead.

BEL. My husband is dead?

TOI. Alas! yes; the poor soul is gone.

BEL. Are you quite certain?

TOI. Quite certain. Nobody knows of it yet. I was all alone here when it happened. He has just breathed his last in my arms. Here, just look at him, full-length in his chair.

BEL. Heaven be praised. I am delivered from a most grievous burden. How silly of you, Toinette, to be so afflicted at his death.

TOI. Ah! Ma'am, I thought I ought to cry.

BEL. Pooh! it is not worth the trouble. What loss is it to anybody, and what good did he do in this world? A wretch, unpleasant to everybody; of nauseous, dirty habits; always a clyster or a dose of physic in his body. Always snivelling, coughing, spitting; a stupid, tedious, ill-natured fellow, who was for ever fatiguing people and scolding night and day at his maids and servants.

TOI. An excellent funeral oration!

BEL. Toinette, you must help me to carry out my design; and you may depend upon it that I will make it worth your while if you serve me. Since, by good luck, nobody is aware of his death, let us put him into his bed, and keep the secret until I have done what I want. There are some papers and some money I must possess myself of. It is not right that I should have passed the best years of my life with him without any kind of advantage. Come along, Toinette, first of all, let us take all the keys.

ARG. (*getting up hastily*). Softly.

BEL. Ah!

ARG. So, my wife, it is thus you love me?

TOI. Ah! the dead man is not dead.

ARG. (*to* BELINE, *who goes away*) I am very glad to see how you love me, and to have heard the noble panegyric you made upon me. This is a good warning, which will make me wise for the future, and prevent me from doing many things.

SCENE XIX. BERALDE (*coming out of the place where he was hiding*), ARGAN, TOINETTE.

BER. Well, brother, you see....

TOI. Now, really, I could never have believed such a thing. But I hear your daughter coming, place yourself as you were just now, and let us see how she will receive the news. It is not a bad thing to try; and since you have begun, you will be able by this means to know the sentiments of your family towards you.

SCENE XX. ARGAN, ANGELIQUE, TOINETTE.

TOI. (*pretending not to see* ANGELIQUE). O heavens! what a sad accident! What an unhappy day!

ANG. What ails you, Toinette, and why do you cry?

TOI. Alas! I have such sad news for you.

ANG. What is it?

TOI. Your father is dead.

ANG. My father is dead, Toinette?

TOI. Yes, just look at him there; he died only a moment ago of a fainting fit that came over him.

ANG. O heavens! what a misfortune! What a cruel grief! Alas I why must I lose my father, the only being left me in the world? and why should I lose him, too, at a time when he was angry with me? What will become of me, unhappy girl that I am? What consolation can I find after so great a loss?

SCENE XXI. ARGAN, ANGELIQUE, CLEANTE, TOINETTE.

CLE. What is the matter with you, dear Angelique, and what misfortune makes you weep?

ANG. Alas! I weep for what was most dear and most precious to me. I weep for the death of my father.

CLE. O heaven! what a misfortune! What an unforeseen stroke of fortune! Alas! after I had asked your uncle to ask you in marriage, I was coming to see him, in order to try by my respect and entreaties to incline his heart to grant you to my wishes.

ANG. Ah! Cleante, let us talk no more of this. Let us give up all hopes of marriage. Now my father is dead, I will have nothing to do with the world, and will renounce it for ever. Yes, my dear father, if I resisted your will, I will at least follow out one of your intentions, and will by that make amends for the sorrow I have caused you. (*Kneeling*) Let me, father, make you this promise here, and kiss you as a proof of my repentance.

ARG. (*kissing* ANGELIQUE). Ah! my daughter!

ANG. Ah!

ARG. Come; do not be afraid. I am not dead. Ah! you are my true flesh and blood and my real daughter, I am delighted to have discovered your good heart.

SCENE XXII. ARGAN, BERALDE, ANGELIQUE, CLEANTE, TOINETTE.

ANG. Ah! what a delightful surprise! Father, since heaven has given you back to our love, let me here throw myself at your feet to implore one favour of you. If you do not approve of what my heart feels, if you refuse to give me Cleante for a husband, I conjure you, at least, not to force me to marry another. It is all I have to ask of you.

CLE. (*throwing himself at* ARGAN'S *feet*). Ah! Sir, allow your heart to be touched by her entreaties and by mine, and do not oppose our mutual love.

BER. Brother, how can you resist all this?

TOI. Will you remain insensible before such affection?

ARG. Well, let him become a doctor, and I will consent to the marriage. (*To* CLEANTE) Yes, turn doctor, Sir, and I will give you my daughter.

CLE. Very willingly, Sir, if it is all that is required to become your son-in-law. I will turn doctor; apothecary also, if you like. It is not such a difficult thing after all, and I would do much more to obtain from you the fair Angelique.

BER. But, brother, it just strikes me; why don't you turn doctor yourself? It would be much more convenient to have all you want within yourself.

TOI. Quite true. That is the very way to cure yourself. There is no disease bold enough to dare to attack the person of a doctor.

ARG. I imagine, brother, that you are laughing at me. Can I study at my age?

BER. Study! What need is there? You are clever enough for that; there are a great many who are not a bit more clever than you are.

ARG. But one must be able to speak Latin well, and know the different diseases and the remedies they require.

BER. When you put on the cap and gown of a doctor, all that will come of itself, and you will afterwards be much more clever than you care to be.

ARG. What! We understand how to discourse upon diseases when we have that dress?

BER. Yes; you have only to hold forth; when you have a cap and gown, any stuff becomes learned, and all rubbish good sense.

TOI. Look you, Sir; a beard is something in itself; a beard is half the doctor.

CLE. Anyhow, I am ready for everything.

BER. (*to* ARGAN). Shall we have the thing done immediately?

ARG. How, immediately?

BER. Yes, in your house.

ARG. In my house?

BER. Yes, I know a body of physicians, friends of mine, who will come presently, and will perform the ceremony in your hall. It will cost you nothing.

ARG. But what can I say, what can I answer?

BER. You will be instructed in a few words, and they will give you in writing all you have to say. Go and dress yourself directly, and I will send for them.

ARG. Very well; let it be done.

SCENE XXIII. BERALDE, ANGELIQUE, CLEANTE.

CLE. What is it yon intend to do, and what do you mean by this body of physicians?

TOI. What is it you are going to do?

BER. To amuse ourselves a little to-night. The players have made a doctor's admission the subject of an interlude, with dances and music. I want everyone to enjoy it, and my brother to act the principal part in it.

ANG. But, uncle, it seems to me that you are making fun of my father.

BER. But, niece, it is not making too much fun of him to fall in with his fancies. We may each of us take part in it ourselves, and thus perform the comedy for each other's amusement. Carnival time authorises it. Let us go quickly and get everything ready.

CLE. (*to* ANGELIQUE). Do you consent to it?

ANG. Yes; since my uncle takes the lead.

THIRD INTERLUDE.

[Footnote: This piece is composed of a mixture of dog-Latin, French, &c. and is utterly untranslateable.]

BURLESQUE CEREMONY *representing the Admission of* MR. GERONTE *to the Degree of Doctor of Medicine.*

First Entry of the BALLET.

PRAESES.
Savantissimi doctores,
Medicinae professores,

101

Qui hic assemblati estis;
Et vos, altri messiores,
Sententiarum Facultatis
Fideles executores,
Chirurgiani et apothicari
Atque tota compagnia aussi,
Salus, honor et argentum,
Atque bonum appetitum.

Non possum, docti confreri,
En moi satis admirari
Qualis bona inventio
Est medici professio;
Quam bella chosa est et bene trovata.
Medicina illa benedicta,
Quae, suo nomine solo,
Surprenanti miraculo,
Depuis si longo tempore,
Facit a gogo vivere
Tant de gens omni genere.

Per totam terram videmus
Grandam vogam ubi sumus;
Et quod grandes et petiti
Sunt de nobis infatuti.
Totus mundus, currens ad nostros remedios,
Nos regardat sicut deos;
Et nostris ordonnanciis
Principes et reges soumissos videtis.

Doncque il est nostrae sapientiae,
Boni sensus atque prudentiae,
De fortement travaillare
A nos bene conservare
In tali credito, voga, et honore;
Et prendere gardam a non recevere
In nostro docto corpore,

Quam personas capabiles,
Et totas dignas remplire
Has placas honorabiles.

C'est pour cela que nunc convocati estis:
Et credo quod trovabitis
Dignam matieram medici
In savanti homine que voici;
Lequel, in chosis omnibus,
Dono ad interrogandum,
Et a fond examinandum
Vostris capacitatibus.

PRIMUS DOCTOR.
Si mihi licentiam dat dominus praeses,
Et tanti docti doctores,
Et assistantes illustres,
Tres savanti bacheliero,
Quem estimo et honoro,
Domandabo causam et rationom quare
Opium facit dormire.

BACHELIERUS.
Mihi a docto doctore
Domandatur causam et rationem quare
Opium facit dormire.
A quoi respondeo,
Quia est in eo
Vertus dormitiva,
Cujus eat natura
Sensus assoupire.

CHORUS.
Bene, bene, bene, bene respondere.
Dignus, dignus est intrare
In nostro docto corpore.
Bene, bene respondere.

SECUNDUS DOCTOR.

Proviso quod non displiceat,

Domino praesidi, lequel n'est pas fat,

Me benigne annuat,

Cum totis doctoribus savantibus,

Et assistantibus bienveillantibus,

Dicat mihi un peu dominus praetendens,

Raison a priori et evidens

Cur rhubarba et le sene

Per nos semper est ordonne

Ad purgandum l'utramque bile?

Si dicit hoc, erit valde habile.

BACHELIERUS.

A docto doctore mihi, qui sum praetendens,

Domandatur raison a priori et evidens

Cur rhubarba et le sene

Per nos semper est ordonne

Ad purgandum l'utramque bile?

Respondeo vobis,

Quia est in illis

Vertus purgativa,

Cujus est natura

Istas duas biles evacuare.

CHORUS.

Bene, bene, bone, bene respondere,

Dignus, dignus est intrare

In nostro docto corpore.

TERTIUS DOCTOR.

Ex responsis, il parait jam sole clarius

Quod lepidum iste caput bachelierus

Non passavit suam vitam ludendo au trictrac,

Nec in prenando du tabac;

Sed explicit pourquoi furfur macrum et parvum lac,

Cum phlebotomia et purgatione humorum,

Appellantur a medisantibus idolae medicorum,
Nec non pontus asinorum?
Si premierement grata sit domino praesidi
Nostra libertas quaestionandi,
Pariter dominis doctribus
Atque de tous ordres benignis auditoribus.

BACHELIERUS.
Quaerit a me dominus doctor
Chrysologos, id est, qui dit d'or,
Quare parvum lac et furfur macrum,
Phlebotomia et purgatio humorum
Appellantur a medisantibus idolae medicorum,
Atque pontus asinorum.
Respondeo quia:
Ista ordonnando non requiritur magna scientia,
Et ex illis quatuor rebus
Medici faciunt ludovicos, pistolas, et des quarts d'ecus.

CHORUS.
Bene, bene, bene, bene respondere
Dignus, dignus est intrare
In nostro docto corpore.

QUARTUS DOCTOR.
Cum permissione domini praesidis,
Doctissimae Facultatis,
Et totius his nostris actis
Companiae assistantis,
Domandabo tibi, docte bacheliere,
Quae sunt remedia
Tam in homine quam in muliere
Quae, in maladia
Ditta hydropisia,
In malo caduco, apoplexia, convulsione et paralysia,
Convenit facere.

BACHELIERUS.

Clysterium donare,
Postea seignare,
Ensuita purgare.

CHORUS.
Bene, bene, bene, bene respondere.
Dignus, dignus est intrare
In nostro docto corpore.

QUINTUS DOCTOR.
Si bonum semblatur domino praesidi.
Doctissimae Facultati,
Et companiae ecoutanti,
Domandabo tibi, erudite bacheliere,
Ut revenir un jour a la maison gravis aegre
Quae remedia colicosis, fievrosis,
Maniacis, nefreticis, freneticis,
Melancolicis, demoniacis,
Asthmaticis atque pulmonicis,
Catharrosis, tussicolisis,
Guttosis, ladris atque gallosis,
In apostemasis plagis et ulcere,
In omni membro demis aut fracture
Convenit facere.

BACHELIERUS.
Clysterium donare,
Postea seignare,
Ensuita purgare.

CHORUS.
Bene, bene, bene, bene respondere.
Dignus, dignus est intrare
In nostro docto corpore.

SEXTUS DOCTOR.
Cum bona venia reverendi praesidis,
Filiorum Hippocratis,

Et totius coronae nos admirantis,
Petam tibi, resolute bacheliere,
Non indignus alumnus di Monspeliere,
Quae remedia caecis, surdis, mutis,
Manchotis, claudis, atque omnibus estropiatis,
Pro coris pedum, malum de dentibus, pesta, rabie,
Et nimis magna commotione in omni novo marie
Convenit facere.

BACHELIERUS.
Clysterium donare,
Postea seignare,
Ensuita purgare.

CHORUS.
Bene, bene, bene, bene respondere.
Dignus, dignus est intrare
In nostro docto corpore.

SEPTIMUS DOCTOR.
Super illas maladias,
Dominus bachelierus dixit maravillas;
Mais, si non ennuyo doctissimam facultatem
Et totam honorabilem companiam
Tam corporaliter quam mentaliter hic praesentem,
Faciam illi unam quaestionem;
De hiero maladus unus
Tombavit in meas manus,
Homo qualitatis et dives comme un Cresus.
Habet grandam fievram cum redoublamentis,
Grandam dolorem capitis,
Cum troublatione spirii et laxamento ventris.
Grandum insuper malum au cote,
Cum granda difficultate
Et pena a respirare;
Veuillas mihi dire,
Docte bacheliere,

Quid illi facere.

BACHELIERUS

Clysterium donare,

Postea seignare,

Ensuita purgare.

CHORUS.

Bene, bene, bene, bene respondere.

Dignus, dignus est intrare

In nostro docto corpore.

IDEM DOCTOR.

Mais, si maladia

Opiniatria

Ponendo modicum a quia

Non vult se guarire,

Quid illi facere?

BACHELIERUS.

Clysterium donare,

Postea seignare,

Ensuita purgare,

Reseignare, repurgare, et reclysterizare.

CHORUS.

Bene, bene, bene, bene respondere.

Dignus, dignus est intrare

In nostro docto corpore.

OCTAVUS DOCTOR.

Impetro favorabile conge

A domino praeside,

Ab electa trouppa doctorum,

Tam practicantium quam practica avidorum,

Et a curiosa turba badodorum.

Ingeniose bacheliere

Qui non potuit esse jusqu'ici deferre,

Faciam tibi unam questionem de importantia.

Messiores, detur nobis audiencia.

Isto die bene mane,

Paulo ante mon dejeune,

Venit ad me una domicella

Italiana jadis bella,

Et ut penso encore un peu pucella,

Quae habebat pallidos colores,

Fievram blancam dicunt magis fini doctores,

Quia plaigniebat se de migraina,

De curta halena,

De granda oppressione,

Jambarum enflatura, et effroyebili lassitudine;

De batimento cordis,

De strangulamento matris,

Alio nomine vapor hysterique,

Quae, sicut omnes maladiae terminatae en ique,

Facit a Galien la nique.

Visagium apparebat bouffietum, et coloris

Tantum vertae quantum merda anseris.

Ex pulsu petito valde frequens, et urina mala

Quam apportaverat in fiola

Non videbatur exempta de febricules;

Au reste, tam debilis quod venerat

De son grabat

In cavallo sur une mule,

Non habuerat menses suos

Ab illa die qui dicitur des grosses eaux;

Sed contabat mihi a l'oreille

Che si non era morta, c'etait grand merveille,

Perche in suo negotio

Era un poco d'amore, et troppo di cordoglio;

Che suo galanto sen era andato in Allemagna,

Servire al signor Brandeburg una campagna.

Usque ad maintenant multi charlatani,

Medici, apothicari, et chirurgiani

Pro sua maladia in veno travaillaverunt,

Juxta meme las novas gripas istius bouru Van Helmont,
Amploiantes ab oculis cancri, ad Alcahest;
Veuillas mihi dire quid superest,
Juxta orthodoxos, illi facere.

BACHELIERUS
Clysterium donare,
Postea seignare,
Ensuita purgare.

CHORUS.
Bene, bene, bene, bene respondero.
Dignus, dignus est intrare
In nostro docto corpore.

IDEM DOCTOR.
Mais si tam grandum couchamentum
Partium naturalium,
Mortaliter obstinatum,
Per clysterium donare,
Seignare
Et reiterando cent fois purgare,
Non potest se guarire,
Finaliter quid trovaris a propos illi facere?

BACHELIERUS
In nomine Hippocratis benedictam cum bono
Garcone conjunctionem imperare.

PRAESES.
Juras gardare statuta
Per Facultatem praescripta,
Cum sensu et jugeamento?

BACHELIERUS.
Juro.
[Footnote: It is said that it was when uttering this word that Moliere
gave way to the illness from which he had long suffered.]

PRAESES.

Essere in Omnibus

Consultationibus

Ancieni aviso,

Aut bono,

Aut mauvaiso!

BACHELIERUS.

Juro.

PRAESES.

De non jamais te servire

De remediis aucunis,

Quam de ceuz seulement almae Facultatis,

Maladus dut-il crevare,

Et mori de suo malo?

BACHELIERUS.

Juro.

PRAESES.

Ego, cum isto boneto

Venerabili et docto,

Dono tibi et concedo

Puissanciam, vertutem atque licentiam

Medicinam cum methodo faciendi

Id est,

Clysterizandi,

Seignandi,

Purgandi,

Sangsuandi,

Ventousandi,

Sacrificandi,

Percandi,

Taillandi,

Coupandi,

Trepanandi,

Brulandi,

Uno verbo, selon les formes, atque impune occidendi

Parisiis et per totem terram;

Rendes, Domine, his messioribus gratiam.

Second Entry of the BALLET.

All the DOCTORS *and* APOTHECARIES *come and do him reverence.*

BACHELIERUS.

Grandes doctres doctrinae

De la rhubarbe et du sene

Ce seroit sans douta a moi chosa folla,

Inepta et ridicula,

Si j'alloibam m'engageare

Vobis louangeas donare,

Et entreprenoibam ajoutare

Des lumieras au soleillo,

Des etoilas au cielo,

Des flammas a l'inferno

Des ondas a l'oceano,

Et des rosas au printano.

Agreate qu'avec uno moto,

Pro toto remercimento,

Rendam gratias corpori tam docto.

Vobis, vobis debeo

Bien plus qu'a nature et qu'a patri meo:

Natura et pater meus

Hominem me habent factum;

Mais vos me (ce qui est bien plus)

Avetis factum medicum

Honor, favor et gratia,

Qui, in hoc corde que voila,

Imprimant ressentimenta

Qui dureront in secula.

CHORUS.

Vivat, vivat, vivat, vivat, cent fois vivat,

Novus doctor, qui tam bene parlat!
Mille, mille annis, et manget et bibat,
Et seignet et tuat!

Third Entry of the BALLET.

All the DOCTORS *and* APOTHECARIES *dance to the sound of*
instruments and voices, the clapping of hands, and the beating
of APOTHECARIES' *mortars.*

CHIRURGUS.
Puisse-t-il voir doctas
Suas ordonnancias,
Omnium chirurgorum,
Et apothicarum
Remplire boutiquas!

CHORUS.
Vivat, vivat, vivat, vivat, cent fois vivat,
Novus doctor, qui tam bene parlat!
Mille, mille annis, et manget et bibat,
Et seignet et tuat!

APOTHICARIUS.
Puissent toti anni
Lui essere boni
Et favorabiles
Et n'habere jamais
Entre ses mains, pestas, epidemias
Quae sunt malas bestias;
Mais semper pluresias, pulmonias
In renibus et vessia pierras,
Rhumatismos d'un anno, et omnis generis fievras,
Fluxus de sanguine, gouttas diabolicas,
Mala de sancto Joanne, Poitevinorum colicas
Scorbutum de Hollandia, verolas parvas et grossas
Bonos chancros atque longas callidopissas.

BACHELIERUS.

Amen.

CHORUS.

Vivat, vivat, vivat, vivat, cent fois vivat,
Novus doctor, qui tam bene parlat!
Mille, mille annis, et manget et bibat,
Et seignet et tuat!

Fourth Entry of the BALLET.

All the DOCTORS *and* APOTHECARIES *go out according to
their rank, as they came in.*

THE END.